Basic Scientific English:
Starting with Newspaper Articles 2

ニュース記事で学ぶやさしい科学英語 2

Osamu Kito & Kazuya Yasuhara

EIHŌSHA

は　し　が　き

　本書は、The Japan Times の社説（Editorials）に掲載された科学的な内容を含む英文記事の中から、近年注目を浴びている 13 種類の現代的なトピックを厳選し、これらをベースとして、科学英語への入門が図れるように教材加工された、初級者向けのリーディング・テキストです。目次にも示されるように、本書では、「人工知能」「認知症」「臓器移植」「異常気象」「野生動物」「再生可能エネルギー」など、私たちの身近に存在している科学的な話題を取り上げていますので、入門レベルの科学的な英文読解能力の養成に、特に適した教材であると言うことができます。また、The Japan Times の社説から取られた英文は、基本的にアカデミック・ライティングで書かれていますので、英文それ自体としても、それなりの読み応えがあり、この意味でも、科学的な英文読解能力のさらなる向上につながるものと考えられます。本書の学習を通して、科学英語へのアクセスが少しでも容易になっていくことを、心より願っております。

　各ユニットの構成は、下記の通りとなります。

Reading Passage
段落ごとに Words, Phrases, Comprehension という 3 つの学習項目を設定していますので、読解英文の細部にわたるまで、しっかりと学習していくことができます。

Dictation
音声学習の一環として、また読解教材の復習として、単語レベルの書き取り問題を設定しました。

Useful Phrases
英文和訳を通して、科学英語でよく用いられる英語の基本的なフレーズを学習していくことができます。

Vocabulary Building
科学領域に関連する名詞レベルの重要フレーズを、日英対照式で学習していくことができます。英語フレーズ力の増強にお役立てください。

　最後に、本書の出版に向けて多大なるご尽力を頂きました、英宝社編集部の皆様に、この場を借りて、感謝申し上げたいと思います。

　2020 年 4 月　名古屋にて

編著者一同

3

目　　次

Unit 1

Artificial Intelligence

Reading Passage

[1]

AI is shorthand for an amalgam of computer processes that permit machines to evaluate and learn about their environment on their own. It includes automated intelligence, assisted intelligence, augmented intelligence and autonomous intelligence. AI depends on huge amounts of data and fast processors that allow real-time analysis to identify patterns. AI will "learn" exponentially as capabilities develop. That means that the occasional stunning feats of AI that we now encounter — victories by machines over chess or go masters — are trivial in comparison to what is coming. One study estimates that AI could contribute up to $15.7 trillion to the global economy by 2030, a boost of 14 percent that will come from productivity gains and shifts in consumer behavior. Another analysis anticipates that AI will boost Japan's annual growth rate by 1.9 percentage points by 2035.

[2]

Russian President Vladimir Putin spoke for many world leaders and AI experts when he told students last year that "artificial intelligence is the future, not only for Russia, but for all humankind," adding that "whoever becomes the leader in this sphere will become the ruler of the world."

【184 words—*The Japan Times* (MAR 1, 2018)】

[Note] Vladimir Putin：ウラジーミル・プーチン

[1]

AI is shorthand for an amalgam of computer processes that permit machines to evaluate and learn about their environment on their own. It includes automated intelligence, assisted intelligence, augmented intelligence and autonomous intelligence. AI depends on huge amounts of data and fast processors that allow real-time analysis to identify patterns. AI will "learn" exponentially as capabilities develop. That means that the occasional stunning feats of AI that we now encounter — victories by machines over chess or go masters — are trivial in comparison to what is coming. One study estimates that AI could contribute up to $15.7 trillion to the global economy by 2030, a boost of 14 percent that will come from productivity gains and shifts in consumer behavior. Another analysis anticipates that AI will boost Japan's annual growth rate by 1.9 percentage points by 2035.

[**Words**] 下記の語彙について、その意味を調べましょう。

	語彙	品詞	意味
1	amalgam	名詞	
2	evaluate	動詞	
3	processor	名詞	
4	identify	動詞	
5	exponentially	副詞	
6	capability	名詞	
7	occasional	形容詞	
8	stunning	形容詞	
9	feat	名詞	
10	encounter	動詞	
11	victory	名詞	
12	trivial	形容詞	
13	estimate	動詞	
14	shift	名詞	
15	analysis	名詞	
16	anticipate	動詞	
17	boost	動詞	

	フレーズ	意味
1	be shorthand for ~	
2	permit X to *do*	
3	on their own	
4	automated intelligence	
5	assisted intelligence	
6	augmented intelligence	
7	autonomous intelligence	
8	depend on ~	
9	huge amounts of data	
10	allow X to *do*	
11	real-time analysis	
12	chess or go masters	
13	in comparison to ~	
14	what is coming	
15	up to $15.7 trillion	
16	the global economy	
17	a boost of 14 percent	
18	productivity gains	
19	consumer behavior	
20	Japan's annual growth rate	
21	1.9 percentage points	

［**Comprehension**］本文に即して、下記の問いに答えましょう。

1. AI（Artificial Intelligence）とは、どのようなものですか。下記の空欄にふさわしい語句を入れましょう。

「機械が自らでその環境を（ ① ）したり、その環境について（ ② ）したりすることを可能とする（ ③ ）のこと。」

①	
②	
③	

2. 本文に書かれていない内容を、下記からすべて選びましょう。

(a) AI には自律知能や支援知能が含まれる。

(b) AI は、大量のデータと高速プロセッサーに依存することで、パターンの同定を可能にしてくれる。

(c) 囲碁において、AI がプロ棋士に勝利することが時々起こっている。

(d) ある研究では、AI は 2030 年までに、最大で 1570 億ドル、世界経済

に貢献していくだろうと推測されている。

(e) AIは生産性を向上させ、消費者行動を変化させると、ある研究では予測されている。

(f) ある研究では、AIが2035年までに日本の食料自給率を1.9％、高めることになるだろうと期待されている。

【第2段落】

[2]

Russian President Vladimir Putin spoke for many world leaders and AI experts when he told students last year that "artificial intelligence is the future, not only for Russia, but for all humankind," adding that "whoever becomes the leader in this sphere will become the ruler of the world."

[Words] 下記の語彙について、その意味を調べましょう。

	語彙	品詞	意味
1	Russian	形容詞	
2	president	名詞	
3	expert	名詞	
4	humankind	名詞	
5	add	動詞	
6	sphere	名詞	
7	ruler	名詞	

[Phrases] 下記のフレーズについて、その意味を調べましょう。

	フレーズ	意味
1	spoke for ~	
2	world leaders	
3	artificial intelligence	

[Comprehension] 本文に即して、下記の問いに答えましょう。

1. AIに関するプーチン大統領の見解として適切なものを、下記から1つ選びましょう。

　　(a) 人工知能研究の分野において、ロシア以上に秀でた国はなく、今やこ

の領域でリーダーとなったロシアは、世界の支配者になることだろう。

(b) 人工知能はロシアのためだけではなく、全人類のための未来でもあるので、人工知能研究の分野では世界中の国々が共同研究に協力するべきである。

(c) ロシアにおける人工知能研究は、全人類の未来に寄与するものであり、国家レベルで人工知能研究に力を注いでいくべきである。

(d) 人工知能はロシアのためだけではなく、全人類のための未来であり、この領域でリーダーになるものは誰でも、世界の支配者になることだろう。

Dictation

※音声を聞いて、語彙を書き取りましょう。

[1]

TRACK No. 2

AI is shorthand for an amalgam of computer processes that permit machines to evaluate and learn about their environment (^{1}⎽⎽⎽⎽⎽) their own. It (^{2}⎽⎽⎽⎽⎽) automated intelligence, assisted intelligence, augmented intelligence and autonomous intelligence. AI depends on huge (^{3}⎽⎽⎽⎽⎽) of data and fast processors that allow real-time analysis to identify patterns. AI will "learn" exponentially (^{4}⎽⎽⎽⎽⎽) capabilities develop. That means that the occasional stunning feats of AI that we now encounter — victories by machines (^{5}⎽⎽⎽⎽⎽) chess or go masters — are trivial in comparison to what is coming. One study (^{6}⎽⎽⎽⎽⎽) that AI could contribute up to $15.7 trillion to the global economy by 2030, a boost of 14 percent that will come from productivity gains and shifts in consumer (^{7}⎽⎽⎽⎽⎽). Another analysis anticipates that AI will boost Japan's annual growth rate by 1.9 percentage points (^{8}⎽⎽⎽⎽⎽) 2035.

[2]

TRACK No. 3

Russian President Vladimir Putin spoke (^{9}⎽⎽⎽⎽⎽) many world leaders and AI experts when he told students last year that "artificial intelligence is the future, not only for Russia, (^{10}⎽⎽⎽⎽⎽) for all humankind," adding that "whoever becomes the leader in this sphere will become the ruler of the world."

【184 words—*The Japan Times* (MAR 1, 2018)】

Useful Phrases

※下線部に留意しながら、下記の英文を和訳しましょう。

TRACK No. 4

1. The values of *x* and *y* are 0.2 and 1.5, respectively.

2. Add a few drops of lemon juice to the water.

3. These experiments were conducted under the same conditions.

Vocabulary Building

※音声を聞いて、フレーズを完成させましょう。その上で、そのフレーズが意味しているものを線で結びましょう。

TRACK No. 5

1. a ( ) ( )	・	・	低脂肪乳
2. ( ) ( )	・	・	左脳
3. a ( ) ( )	・	・	発電所
4. ( ) ( )	・	・	光エネルギー
5. a ( ) ( )	・	・	デジタルカメラ
6. an ( )	・	・	飲料水
7. the ( ) ( )	・	・	地震
8. ( )-( ) ( )	・	・	国立公園

Unit 2

Dementia

Reading Passage

[1]

Dementia, a progressive neurological condition that tends to affect more people as they advance in age, has been linked to abnormalities in brain cells as well as lifestyle-related diseases such as diabetes and arteriosclerosis, but no cure has been established for the illness. Alzheimer's is said to be the most prevalent type of dementia, affecting two-thirds of all patients, but the medicines currently available only slow the progression of the patients' conditions.

[2]

There were an estimated 4.62 million patients in 2012, along with 4 million others who suffer from light cognitive disorders and have a risk of developing dementia symptoms, according to the health ministry.

[3]

In recent years, there have been alarming reports of dementia sufferers going missing after wandering away from their homes. Roughly 10,000 such cases are reported each year. Increasingly reports of patients falling victim to accidents and consumer-related fraud also have been highlighted as serious social problems.

[4]

The issue of people quitting jobs to care for their elderly relatives suffering from dementia has come to the fore, along with an increase in the number of younger-generation people developing the symptoms.

【184 words—*The Japan Times* (FEB 5, 2015)】

[1]

Dementia, a progressive neurological condition that tends to affect more people as they advance in age, has been linked to abnormalities in brain cells as well as lifestyle-related diseases such as diabetes and arteriosclerosis, but no cure has been established for the illness. Alzheimer's is said to be the most prevalent type of dementia, affecting two-thirds of all patients, but the medicines currently available only slow the progression of the patients' conditions.

[**Words**] 下記の語彙について、その意味を調べましょう。

	語彙	品詞	意味
1	dementia	名詞	
2	progressive	形容詞	
3	affect	動詞	
4	advance	動詞	
5	abnormality	名詞	
6	diabetes	名詞	
7	arteriosclerosis	名詞	
8	cure	名詞	
9	establish	動詞	
10	Alzheimer's	名詞	
11	prevalent	形容詞	
12	medicine	名詞	
13	currently	副詞	
14	available	形容詞	
15	progression	名詞	
16	condition	名詞	

[**Phrases**] 下記のフレーズについて、その意味を調べましょう。

	フレーズ	意味
1	a neurological condition	
2	tend to *do*	
3	be linked to ~	
4	brain cells	
5	lifestyle-related diseases	
6	be said to *do*	
7	two-thirds of ~	

[**Comprehension**] 本文に即して、下記の問いに答えましょう。

1. 本文には書かれていない内容を、下記からすべて選びましょう。

    (a) 認知症は、年齢を重ねていくことで多くの患者が発生してくる傾向にある。

    (b) 認知症は、進行性の脳疾患である。

    (c) 認知症は、筋細胞の異常と関連づけられており、治療法が確立していない。

    (d) 認知症の全患者の 2/3 を占めているのは、アルツハイマー病である。

    (e) アルツハイマー病に対する根治療法は、今のところ、確立されていない。

【第2段落】

---

[2]

There were an estimated 4.62 million patients in 2012, along with 4 million others who suffer from light cognitive disorders and have a risk of developing dementia symptoms, according to the health ministry.

[**Words**] 下記の語彙について、その意味を調べましょう。

	語彙	品詞	意味
1	light	形容詞	
2	develop	動詞	
3	symptom	名詞	

[**Phrases**] 下記のフレーズについて、その意味を調べましょう。

	フレーズ	意味
1	an estimated 4.62 million patients	
2	along with ~	
3	suffer from ~	
4	cognitive disorders	
5	according to ~	
6	the health ministry	

[**Comprehension**] 本文に即して、下記の問いに答えましょう。

1. 本文に書かれている内容と合致するものを、1つ選びましょう。

    (a) 2012 年の時点で、推定で 462 万人の認知症患者がいることにくわえて、認知症の症状へと発展していく恐れがある軽い認知障害を発症している患者も 400 万人いると言われている。

    (b) 2012 年の時点で、軽い認知障害を発症している患者が推定で 462 万人おり、そのうちの 400 万人がアルツハイマー病を発症する恐れがあると言われている。

    (c) 2012 年の時点で、推定で 462 万人の認知症患者がおり、そのうちの 400 万人がアルツハイマー病に罹患していると言われている。

    (d) 2012 年の時点で、推定で 462 万人の脳疾患の患者がおり、そのうちの 400 万人が認知症の症状へと発展していく恐れがある軽い認知障害に罹患していると言われている。

【第 3 段落】

[3]

In recent years, there have been alarming reports of dementia sufferers going missing after wandering away from their homes. Roughly 10,000 such cases are reported each year. Increasingly reports of patients falling victim to accidents and consumer-related fraud also have been highlighted as serious social problems.

[**Words**] 下記の語彙について、その意味を調べましょう。

	語彙	品詞	意味
1	alarming	形容詞	
2	report	名詞	
3	sufferer	名詞	
4	wander	動詞	
5	roughly	副詞	
6	increasingly	副詞	
7	highlight	動詞	

	フレーズ	意味
1	in recent years	
2	go missing	
3	away from ～	
4	each year	
5	fall victim to ～	
6	consumer-related fraud	
7	serious social problems	

[**Comprehension**] 本文に即して、下記の問いに答えましょう。

1. 本文中の "Roughly 10,000 such cases"（2行目）とは、具体的に何を指しているますか。正しい答えを、下記から1つ選びましょう。

(a) 高齢者が、家を出てから徘徊した挙句、認知症と診断されてしまうケース。

(b) 認知症患者が、家を出てから徘徊した挙句、行方不明となってしまうケース。

(c) 認知症患者が、事故や消費者関連詐欺の犠牲となってしまうケース。

(d) 認知症患者が、家を出てから行方不明になってしまったり、事故や消費者関連詐欺の犠牲となってしまうケース。

【第4段落】

[4]

The issue of people quitting jobs to care for their elderly relatives suffering from dementia has come to the fore, along with an increase in the number of younger-generation people developing the symptoms.

[**Words**] 下記の語彙について、その意味を調べましょう。

	語彙	品詞	意味
1	issue	名詞	
2	quit	動詞	
3	increase	名詞	

[Phrases] 下記のフレーズについて、その意味を調べましょう。

	フレーズ	意味
1	care for ~	
2	elderly relatives	
3	come to the fore	
4	younger-generation people	

[Comprehension] 本文に即して、下記の問いに答えましょう。

1. 認知症を取り巻く問題で、本文には書かれていないものを、すべて選びましょう。

(a) 認知症にかかっている高齢の親族の世話をする目的で、仕事を辞めてしまうこと。

(b) 定年退職後に、認知症にかかっている高齢の親族の世話をしなければならないこと。

(c) 認知症について正しい知識を持っていない若い世代の人々が増加していること。

(d) 認知症の症状を発症してしまうより若い世代の人々が増加していること。

[MEMO]

……………………………………………………………………

……………………………………………………………………

……………………………………………………………………

……………………………………………………………………

……………………………………………………………………

……………………………………………………………………

……………………………………………………………………

……………………………………………………………………

Dictation

※音声を聞いて、語彙を書き取りましょう。

[1]

TRACK No. 6

Dementia, a progressive neurological condition that (^{1}) to affect more people as they advance in age, has been linked to abnormalities in brain cells as well as lifestyle-related (^{2}) such as diabetes and arteriosclerosis, but no cure has been established for the illness. Alzheimer's is said to be the most prevalent type of dementia, affecting (^{3}) of all patients, but the medicines currently available only slow the progression of the patients' conditions.

[2]

TRACK No. 7

There were an estimated 4.62 million patients in 2012, along (^{4}) 4 million others who suffer (^{5}) light cognitive disorders and have a risk of developing dementia symptoms, according to the health ministry.

[3]

TRACK No. 8

In recent years, (^{6}) have been alarming reports of dementia sufferers going missing after wandering away from their homes. Roughly 10,000 such cases are reported each year. Increasingly reports of patients falling (^{7}) to accidents and consumer-related fraud also have been highlighted as serious (^{8}) problems.

[4]

TRACK No. 9

The issue of people (^{9}) jobs to care for their elderly relatives suffering from dementia has come to the fore, along with an increase in (^{10}) number of younger-generation people developing the symptoms.

【184 words—*The Japan Times* (FEB 5, 2015)】

Useful Phrases

TRACK No.10

※下線部に留意しながら、下記の英文を和訳しましょう。

1. These animals are under threat of extinction.

   _____

2. The purpose of this paper is to answer these three questions.

   _____

3. Measure and record the weight of the test tube.

   _____

Vocabulary Building

※音声を聞いて、フレーズを完成させましょう。その上で、そのフレーズが意味しているものを線で結びましょう。

TRACK No. 11

1. a (　　　) (　　　) ・　・ がん細胞
2. a (　　　) (　　　) ・　・ ペットボトル
3. (　　　) (　　　) (　　　) ・　・ 心臓発作
4. (　　　) (　　　) ・　・ 水道管
5. (　　　) (　　　) ・　・ 豆乳
6. a (　　　) (　　　) ・　・ 油田
7. a (　　　) (　　　) ・　・ 体脂肪
8. an (　　　) (　　　) ・　・ 高血圧

Unit 3

◇◇◇◇◇◇◇

A Flu Pandemic

Reading Passage

[1]

The fight to contain a flu pandemic is a race against time. For containment operations by governments and international institutions to be effective, reports of flu virus mutations must be made within two weeks of discovery. To this end an international information network centering around the WHO should be formed. A WHO study reveals that in the roughly 70 human cases of avian flu in China, Vietnam, Cambodia, Indonesia and Thailand, it took an average of 16.7 days for a report to reach the WHO. The study suggests that Japan can do more to help construct information systems that are capable of quickly relaying reports from Asian villages, where the virus is mostly likely to infect humans, to the WHO.

[2]

In Japan, 43 prefectural governments have set up headquarters to counter the avian flu and a possible influenza pandemic. The Health, Welfare and Labor Ministry on Jan. 14 announced a plan to stockpile 25 million courses of Tamiflu, about 1.7 times more than the previous plan. It also raised the maximum death estimate of a flu pandemic from 170,000 to 640,000.

【181 words—*The Japan Times* (JAN 26, 2006)】

[Notes] Tamiflu：タミフル

WHO (World Health Organization)：世界保健機関

[1]

The fight to contain a flu pandemic is a race against time. For containment operations by governments and international institutions to be effective, reports of flu virus mutations must be made within two weeks of discovery. To this end an international information network centering around the WHO should be formed. A WHO study reveals that in the roughly 70 human cases of avian flu in China, Vietnam, Cambodia, Indonesia and Thailand, it took an average of 16.7 days for a report to reach the WHO. The study suggests that Japan can do more to help construct information systems that are capable of quickly relaying reports from Asian villages, where the virus is mostly likely to infect humans, to the WHO.

[**Words**] 下記の語彙について、その意味を調べましょう。

	語彙	品詞	意味
1	contain	動詞	
2	government	名詞	
3	effective	形容詞	
4	virus	名詞	
5	mutation	名詞	
6	form	動詞	
7	reveal	動詞	
8	roughly	副詞	
9	Vietnam	名詞	
10	Cambodia	名詞	
11	Indonesia	名詞	
12	Thailand	名詞	
13	suggest	動詞	
14	construct	動詞	
15	relay	動詞	
16	infect	動詞	

[**Phrases**] 下記のフレーズについて、その意味を調べましょう。

	フレーズ	意味
1	a flu pandemic	
2	a race against time	

3	containment operations	
4	international institutions	
5	within two weeks	
6	to this end	
7	an information network	
8	center around ~	
9	avian flu	
10	an average of 16.7 days	
11	information systems	
12	be capable of *doing*	
13	Asian villages	
14	be mostly likely to *do*	

［**Comprehension**］本文に即して、下記の問いに答えましょう。

1. 本文冒頭に "The fight to contain a flu pandemic is a race against time." とありますが、そのように言えるのはなぜですか。正しい理由を1つ選びましょう。

    (a) インフルエンザウイルスの突然変異は、2週間以内に起こるから。

    (b) インフルエンザウイルスの突然変異が確認された場合、その2週間後にウイルスの世界的蔓延が起こると言われているから。

    (c) インフルエンザウイルスの突然変異が確認された場合、その2週間以内に、WHO にその報告がなされる必要があるから。

    (d) インフルエンザウイルスの突然変異が確認された場合、その2週間以内にそのウイルスのワクチンが開発されなければ、何の効果も期待できないから。

2. 世界保健機関（WHO）による研究が示唆していることとは、次のうちどれですか。1つ選びましょう。

    (a) ウイルスに関する情報を国家間で共有するために、日本を中心とした国際的な情報ネットワークが形成されるべきであること。

    (b) 東南アジア諸国において発生した鳥インフルエンザのヒト感染への症例のうち、約70のものについては、それらの症状が改善するのに、平均で 16.7 日かかったこと。

    (c) ウイルスのヒトへの感染が高まってきているアジアの各地域で、迅速な情報共有のためのシステムを構築していくために、WHO にはもっとできることがあるということ。

(d) アジアの各地域からなされるウイルス感染に関する報告を、迅速に
WHOに中継することができる情報システムを構築していくために、日
本にはもっとできることがあるということ。

【第2段落】

[2]

In Japan, 43 prefectural governments have set up headquarters to counter the avian flu
and a possible influenza pandemic. The Health, Welfare and Labor Ministry on Jan. 14
announced a plan to stockpile 25 million courses of Tamiflu, about 1.7 times more than
the previous plan. It also raised the maximum death estimate of a flu pandemic from
170,000 to 640,000.

[**Words**] 下記の語彙について、その意味を調べましょう。

	語彙	品詞	意味
1	headquarter	名詞	
2	counter	動詞	
3	possible	形容詞	
4	influenza	名詞	
5	pandemic	名詞	
6	announce	動詞	
7	stockpile	動詞	
8	previous	形容詞	
9	raise	動詞	
10	maximum	形容詞	

[**Phrases**] 下記のフレーズについて、その意味を調べましょう。

	フレーズ	意味
1	43 prefectural governments	
2	set up	
3	The Health, Welfare and Labor Ministry	
4	25 million courses of Tamiflu	
5	about 1.7 times	
6	a death estimate	

[**Comprehension**] 本文に即して、下記の問いに答えましょう。

1. 日本では、インフルエンザや鳥インフルエンザの世界的蔓延を阻止するために、どのような対策が取られましたか。下記の空欄にふさわしい語句を入れましょう。

「世界的蔓延を阻止するための（ ① ）が、43都道府県ですでに設置されている。また、厚生労働省によって、従来の計画の約（ ② ）倍の量に相当する（ ③ ）クール分のタミフルを備蓄する計画が発表されている。」

①	
②	
③	

Dictation

※音声を聞いて、語彙を書き取りましょう。

[1]
TRACK No. 12

The fight to (^{1}) a flu pandemic is a race against time. For containment operations by governments and international institutions to be (^{2}), reports of flu virus mutations must be made (^{3}) two weeks of discovery. To this end an international information network centering around the WHO should be (^{4}). A WHO study reveals that in the roughly 70 human cases of avian flu in China, Vietnam, Cambodia, Indonesia and Thailand, it took an (^{5}) of 16.7 days for a report to reach the WHO. The study suggests that Japan can do more to help (^{6}) information systems that are capable (^{7}) quickly relaying reports from Asian villages, where the virus is mostly likely to infect humans, to the WHO.

[2]
TRACK No. 13

In Japan, 43 prefectural governments have set (^{8}) headquarters to counter the avian flu and a possible influenza pandemic. The Health, Welfare and Labor Ministry on Jan. 14 announced a plan to stockpile 25 million courses of Tamiflu, about (^{9}) times more than the previous plan. It also raised the maximum death estimate of a flu pandemic from 170,000 to (^{10}).

【181 words—*The Japan Times* (JAN 26, 2006)】

Useful Phrases

※下線部に留意しながら、下記の英文を和訳しましょう。

TRACK No. 14

1. The diameter of the circle is 2.54 centimeters.

2. These data are summarized in Tables 4-8.

3. This survey was conducted in September 2012.

Vocabulary Building

※音声を聞いて、フレーズを完成させましょう。その上で、そのフレーズが意味しているものを線で結びましょう。

TRACK No. 15

1.	(	) (	) ・	・ 正の数
2.	(	) (	) ・	・ 血液検査
3. a	(	) (	) ・	・ 皮膚がん
4. a	(	) (	) ・	・ 副作用
5.	(	) (	) ・	・ 脳波
6.	(	) (	) ・	・ 口頭発表
7. a	(	) (	) ・	・ 緑茶
8. an	(	) (	) ・	・ 私立大学

Unit 4
World Natural Heritage Sites

Reading Passage

[1]

Pristine subtropical forests of evergreen, broad-leaved trees grace Amami-Oshima and Tokunoshima islands of Kagoshima, Iriomote Island of Okinawa and the northern part of the Yanbaru area of Okinawa Island. These sites cover a total of some 38,000 hectares and their forests are home to rare species. In submitting the proposal to the United Nations Educational, Scientific and Cultural Organization, the government said that these islands, after they were separated from the Asian land mass, saw distinctive evolution, giving rise to a variety of indigenous species such as the Amami rabbit, the Okinawa rail and the Iriomote cat, and that the sites are important from the standpoint of biodiversity due to the existence of these valuable endemic species.

[2]

Given these characteristics, the sites have universal value. UNESCO's World Heritage Committee will decide whether to add them to its list in summer 2018, following on-site inspections. If the sites are put on the list, they will be the fifth area in Japan to receive World Natural Heritage recognition, following the Shirakami mountainous area of Aomori and Akita prefectures, Yaku Island of Kagoshima, the Shiretoko Peninsula in Hokkaido and the Ogasawara Islands of Tokyo.

【191 words—*The Japan Times* (FEB 4, 2017)】

[Note] Yanbaru area：山原エリア

[1]

Pristine subtropical forests of evergreen, broad-leaved trees grace Amami-Oshima and Tokunoshima islands of Kagoshima, Iriomote Island of Okinawa and the northern part of the Yanbaru area of Okinawa Island. These sites cover a total of some 38,000 hectares and their forests are home to rare species.

[**Words**] 下記の語彙について、その意味を調べましょう。

	語彙	品詞	意味
1	pristine	形容詞	
2	grace	動詞	
3	cover	動詞	
4	hectare	名詞	

[**Phrases**] 下記のフレーズについて、その意味を調べましょう。

	フレーズ	意味
1	subtropical forests	
2	evergreen trees	
3	broad-leaved trees	
4	the northern part of ~	
5	a total of some 38,000 hectares	
6	be home to ~	
7	rare species	

[**Comprehension**] 本文に即して、下記の問いに答えましょう。

1. 3行目の "These sites" とは、具体的に何を指していますか。英語ですべて抜き出してみましょう。

In submitting the proposal to the United Nations Educational, Scientific and Cultural Organization, the government said that these islands, after they were separated from the Asian land mass, saw distinctive evolution, giving rise to a variety of indigenous species such as the Amami rabbit, the Okinawa rail and the Iriomote cat, and that the sites are important from the standpoint of biodiversity due to the existence of these valuable endemic species.

［**Words**］下記の語彙について、その意味を調べましょう。

	語彙	品詞	意味
1	submit	動詞	
2	proposal	名詞	
3	government	名詞	
4	distinctive	形容詞	
5	evolution	名詞	
6	biodiversity	名詞	
7	existence	名詞	
8	valuable	形容詞	

［**Phrases**］下記のフレーズについて、その意味を調べましょう。

	フレーズ	意味
1	United Nations Educational, Scientific and Cultural Organization	
2	be separated from ~	
3	the Asian land mass	
4	give rise to ~	
5	a variety of species	
6	indigenous species	
7	the Amami rabbit	
8	the Okinawa rail	
9	the Iriomote cat	
10	from the standpoint of ~	
11	due to ~	
12	endemic species	

[**Comprehension**] 本文に即して、下記の問いに答えましょう。

1. 第1段落の最後にある "these valuable endemic species" とは、具体的には、どのような生物を指していますか。英語ですべて抜き出してみましょう。

2. 下記の記述について、本文の内容と合致していればTを、合致していなければFを、括弧に入れましょう。

    (a) 沖縄県の山原エリア北部は、世界自然遺産に認定されている。（　　　）

    (b) 西表島や山原エリアには、様々な絶滅危惧種の動物が生息している。

      （　　　）

    (c) 日本政府は、西表島や徳之島を世界自然遺産に登録することに関して、積極的ではない。（　　　）

【**第2段落**】 ^{TRACK} No. 17

[2]

Given these characteristics, the sites have universal value. UNESCO's World Heritage Committee will decide whether to add them to its list in summer 2018, following on-site inspections. If the sites are put on the list, they will be the fifth area in Japan to receive World Natural Heritage recognition, following the Shirakami mountainous area of Aomori and Akita prefectures, Yaku Island of Kagoshima, the Shiretoko Peninsula in Hokkaido and the Ogasawara Islands of Tokyo.

[**Words**] 下記の語彙について、その意味を調べましょう。

	語彙	品詞	意味
1	characteristic	名詞	
2	universal	形容詞	

3	recognition	名詞	
4	mountainous	形容詞	
5	prefecture	名詞	
6	peninsula	名詞	

[**Phrases**] 下記のフレーズについて、その意味を調べましょう。

	フレーズ	意味
1	given ~	
2	UNESCO's World Heritage Committee	
3	whether to *do*	
4	add X to Y	
5	in summer 2018	
6	following ~	
7	on-site inspections	
8	World Natural Heritage	
9	a mountainous area	

[**Comprehension**] 本文に即して、下記の問いに答えましょう。

1. この記事が執筆された時点では、日本には世界自然遺産が何カ所あることに
   なりますか。下記より、正しいものを選びましょう。

    (a) 3カ所

    (b) 4カ所

    (c) 5カ所

    (d) 6カ所

Dictation

※音声を聞いて、語彙を書き取りましょう。

[1]

TRACK No. 16

Pristine (¹   ) forests of evergreen, broad-leaved trees grace Amami-Oshima and Tokunoshima islands of Kagoshima, Iriomote Island of Okinawa and the northern part of the Yanbaru area of Okinawa Island. These sites (²   ) a total of some 38,000 hectares and their forests are home to rare (³   ). In submitting the (⁴   ) to the United Nations Educational, Scientific and Cultural Organization, the government said that these islands, after they were separated from the Asian land mass, saw distinctive (⁵   ), giving rise to a variety of indigenous species such as the Amami rabbit, the Okinawa rail and the Iriomote cat, and that the sites are important from the standpoint of (⁶   ) due to the existence of these valuable endemic species.

[2]

TRACK No. 17

(⁷   ) these characteristics, the sites have universal value. UNESCO's World Heritage Committee will decide whether to (⁸   ) them to its list in summer 2018, following on-site inspections. If the sites are put on the list, they will be the (⁹   ) area in Japan to receive World Natural Heritage recognition, following the Shirakami mountainous area of Aomori and Akita prefectures, Yaku Island of Kagoshima, the Shiretoko (¹⁰   ) in Hokkaido and the Ogasawara Islands of Tokyo.

【191 words—*The Japan Times* (FEB 4, 2017)】

[MEMO]

....

....

....

....

Useful Phrases

※下線部に留意しながら、下記の英文を和訳しましょう。

TRACK No. 18

1. This mathematical model was developed by Dr. Richard Johnson.

2. The surface area of the prism is about 25 square centimeters.

3. These substances are very soluble in water.

Vocabulary Building

※音声を聞いて、フレーズを完成させましょう。その上で、そのフレーズが意味しているものを線で結びましょう。

TRACK No. 19

1. a ( ) ( ) ・	・	乳がん
2. ( ) ( ) ・	・	異常気象
3. ( ) ( ) ・	・	望遠鏡
4. the ( ) ( ) ・	・	負の数
5. a ( ) ( ) ・	・	試験管
6. a ( ) ( ) ・	・	沸点
7. a ( ) ・	・	漢方薬
8. ( ) ( ) ・	・	研究論文

Unit 5

◇◇◇◇◇◇◇

Active Volcanoes

Reading Passage

[1]

When Mount Moto-Shirane in Gunma Prefecture erupted without warning Jan. 23, killing one person and injuring 11 others, the Meteorological Agency was unable to issue an alert immediately after the eruption — the first one was issued only about an hour later. The town of Kusatsu, the site of a ski resort near the volcano, only managed to broadcast a disaster warning through a wireless system 50 minutes after the eruption. Along with verifying what happened at the volcano, the agency needs to look into whether the volcano observation and alert system in the area worked. The government and the volcanologist community should re-examine the current monitoring and alert system, and review ways to best respond to eruptions once they have taken place.

[2]

Japan has 111 active volcanoes — accounting for about 7 percent of active volcanoes the world over — and 50 of them are observed round the clock under the Meteorological Agency's volcano monitoring program. The volcanic area where the eruption occurred last week is one of these 50 areas. The Tokyo Institute of Technology has an observatory there, making what happened all the more shocking.

【184 words—*The Japan Times* (JAN 31, 2018)】

[Notes] Mount Moto-Shirane：本白根山
　　　　Kusatsu：草津市

[1]

When Mount Moto-Shirane in Gunma Prefecture erupted without warning Jan. 23, killing one person and injuring 11 others, the Meteorological Agency was unable to issue an alert immediately after the eruption — the first one was issued only about an hour later. The town of Kusatsu, the site of a ski resort near the volcano, only managed to broadcast a disaster warning through a wireless system 50 minutes after the eruption.

［**Words**］下記の語彙について、その意味を調べましょう。

	語彙	品詞	意味
1	prefecture	名詞	
2	erupt	動詞	
3	injure	動詞	
4	issue	動詞	
5	alert	名詞	
6	immediately	副詞	
7	eruption	名詞	
8	volcano	名詞	
9	broadcast	動詞	
10	wireless	形容詞	

［**Phrases**］下記のフレーズについて、その意味を調べましょう。

	フレーズ	意味
1	without warning	
2	the Meteorological Agency	
3	be unable to *do*	
4	about an hour later	
5	a ski resort	
6	manage to *do*	
7	a disaster warning	
8	a wireless system	
9	50 minutes after the eruption	

［**Comprehension**］本文に即して、下記の問いに答えましょう。

1. 本文の内容と合致するものを、すべて選びましょう。

(a) 本白根山の噴火により、死者11名を出すことになった。

(b) 本白根山が噴火する数時間前に、噴火の前兆現象が観察されていた。

(c) 本白根山が噴火してからおよそ1時間後に、警報が発令された。

(d) 本白根山付近の町では、防災無線を通じて、噴火の10分後には警報が伝達された。

2. 3行目に登場する "one" は、何を指していますか。下記から1つ選びましょう。

(a) 噴火

(b) 警報

(c) 報道

(d) 死者

【第1段落（後半）】

Along with verifying what happened at the volcano, the agency needs to look into whether the volcano observation and alert system in the area worked. The government and the volcanologist community should re-examine the current monitoring and alert system, and review ways to best respond to eruptions once they have taken place.

[**Words**] 下記の語彙について、その意味を調べましょう。

	語彙	品詞	意味
1	verify	動詞	
2	observation	名詞	
3	work	動詞	
4	government	名詞	
5	volcanologist	名詞	
6	re-examine	動詞	
7	current	形容詞	
8	monitoring	名詞	
9	review	動詞	

[**Phrases**] 下記のフレーズについて、その意味を調べましょう。

	フレーズ	意味
1	along with ~	
2	look into ~	

3	the volcano observation and alert system	
4	the volcanologist community	
5	respond to ~	
6	take place	

［**Comprehension**］本文に即して、下記の問いに答えましょう。

1. 気象庁や政府がこれから行うべきこととは、どのようなことですか。下記から
すべて選びましょう。

　　(a) 噴火が起こった際に作動する火山監視・警報システムを、新たに開発
　　　　すること。

　　(b) 火山学界と協同して、火山の研究を進めること。

　　(c) 本白根山の噴火の際に、その地域の火山監視・警報システムが作動し
　　　　ていたのかどうかを調査すること。

　　(d) 噴火が起こった際の最善の対処法を見直すこと。

【第2段落】

TRACK No. 21

[2]

Japan has 111 active volcanoes — accounting for about 7 percent of active volcanoes the world over — and 50 of them are observed round the clock under the Meteorological Agency's volcano monitoring program. The volcanic area where the eruption occurred last week is one of these 50 areas. The Tokyo Institute of Technology has an observatory there, making what happened all the more shocking.

［**Words**］下記の語彙について、その意味を調べましょう。

	語彙	品詞	意味
1	observe	動詞	
2	volcanic	形容詞	
3	occur	動詞	
4	observatory	名詞	
5	shocking	形容詞	

[**Phrases**] 下記のフレーズについて、その意味を調べましょう。

	フレーズ	意味
1	an active volcano	
2	account for ~	
3	round the clock	
4	the Meteorological Agency's volcano monitoring program	
5	the Tokyo Institute of Technology	
6	all the more	

[**Comprehension**] 本文に即して、下記の問いに答えましょう。

1. 本文の内容に合わせて、空欄を埋めましょう。なお、（ ② ）と（ ③ ）には、
   数字が入ります。

　　　日本には 111 の（ ① ）が存在し、世界中の（ ① ）のおよそ（ ② ）％を
　　占めている。また、そのうちの（ ③ ）の火山が、気象庁の（ ④ ）によっ
　　て、24 時間体制で観測されている。

①	
②	
③	
④	

Dictation

※音声を聞いて、語彙を書き取りましょう。

[1]

TRACK No. 20

When Mount Moto-Shirane in Gunma Prefecture (^{1}) without warning Jan. 23, killing one person and injuring 11 others, the Meteorological Agency was unable to issue an (^{2}) immediately after the eruption — the first one was issued only about an hour later. The town of Kusatsu, the site of a ski resort near the (^{3}), only managed to broadcast a disaster warning through a wireless system 50 minutes after the eruption. Along with (^{4}) what happened at the volcano, the agency needs to look into whether the volcano (^{5}) and alert system in the area worked. The government and the volcanologist community should re-examine the (^{6}) monitoring and alert system, and review ways to best (^{7}) to eruptions once they have taken place.

[2]

TRACK No. 21

Japan has 111 active volcanoes — (^{8}) for about 7 percent of active volcanoes the world over — and 50 of them are observed round the (^{9}) under the Meteorological Agency's volcano monitoring program. The volcanic area where the eruption occurred last week is one of these 50 areas. The Tokyo Institute of Technology has an (^{10}) there, making what happened all the more shocking.

【184 words—*The Japan Times* (JAN 31, 2018)】

[MEMO]

....

....

....

....

....

Useful Phrases

※下線部に留意しながら、下記の英文を和訳しましょう。

TRACK No. 22

1. The <u>radius of the sphere</u> is 12 centimeters.

2. The energy was released <u>in the form of light</u>.

3. This issue will be discussed <u>in more detail</u> in Chapter 7.

Vocabulary Building

※音声を聞いて、フレーズを完成させましょう。その上で、そのフレーズが意味しているものを線で結びましょう。

TRACK No. 23

1.	the (	) (	) ·	·	静電気
2.		a (	) ·	·	緑色植物
3.	a (	) (	) ·	·	ビーカー
4.	a (	) (	) ·	·	植物園
5.	a (	) (	) ·	·	大気汚染
6.		an (	) ·	·	融点
7.	(	) (	) ·	·	必要条件
8.	(	) (	) ·	·	宇宙飛行士

Unit 6
Japan's Scientific Research

Reading Passage

[1]

In the 150 years since the Meiji Restoration, progress in science and technology has been one of the key driving forces behind Japan's modernization. Today, however, the overall prospect of the nation's scientific research isn't all that promising. While rapid progress is being made in computer science and robotics, various data show that Japan's scientific research is on the verge of stalling. The government, universities and other research institutes must take the situation seriously and take rational steps to address the problem.

[2]

Since 2000, 17 Japanese have received Nobel Prizes in the natural sciences. But because most Nobel laureates receive the honor for what they accomplished 20 to 40 years earlier, such numbers do not necessarily reflect the nation's current scientific power. Conditions of Japan's scientific researchers have in fact deteriorated over the same period. The government's research and development spending has been flat since 2001 while other countries like China, South Korea and Germany have substantially increased their expenditures. In 2004, when the status of national universities was changed to one similar to independent administrative bodies, government grants to them began to fall, with the fiscal 2017 figure 10 percent less than in 2004.

【195 words—*The Japan Times* (JAN 9, 2018)】

[1]

In the 150 years since the Meiji Restoration, progress in science and technology has been one of the key driving forces behind Japan's modernization. Today, however, the overall prospect of the nation's scientific research isn't all that promising.

［**Words**］下記の語彙について、その意味を調べましょう。

	語彙	品詞	意味
1	progress	名詞	
2	science	名詞	
3	technology	名詞	
4	key	形容詞	
5	behind	前置詞	
6	modernization	名詞	
7	overall	形容詞	
8	prospect	名詞	
9	promising	形容詞	

［**Phrases**］下記のフレーズについて、その意味を調べましょう。

	フレーズ	意味
1	the Meiji Restoration	
2	a driving force	
3	scientific research	
4	be not all that ~	

［**Comprehension**］本文に即して、下記の問いに答えましょう。

1. 2行目に登場する "however" は、対比を意味する接続詞ですが、ここで対比されていることとは、どのようなことですか。下記の空欄にふさわしい語句を入れましょう。

「（ ① ）以降の150年間は、（ ② ）の進展が、日本の（ ③ ）における主要な原動力の1つとなってきた」という事実と、「昨今の日本における（ ④ ）の全体的な見通しは、それほど前途有望ではない」という事実。

①	
②	
③	
④	

【第1段落（後半）】

While rapid progress is being made in computer science and robotics, various data show that Japan's scientific research is on the verge of stalling. The government, universities and other research institutes must take the situation seriously and take rational steps to address the problem.

［**Words**］下記の語彙について、その意味を調べましょう。

	語彙	品詞	意味
1	rapid	形容詞	
2	robotics	名詞	
3	various	形容詞	
4	stall	動詞	
5	government	名詞	
6	university	名詞	
7	situation	名詞	
8	seriously	副詞	
9	rational	形容詞	
10	address	動詞	

［**Phrases**］下記のフレーズについて、その意味を調べましょう。

	フレーズ	意味
1	make rapid progress	
2	computer science	
3	be on the verge of ~	
4	a research institute	
5	address the problem	

［**Comprehension**］本文に即して、下記の問いに答えましょう。

1. 3行目の "the situation" とは、どのような状況のことですか。正しい答えを、下記から1つ選びましょう。

(a) 日本のロボット工学やコンピュータ科学の研究において、急速な進展が見られるという状況。

(b) 日本のロボット工学やコンピュータ科学が衰退しつつあるという状況。

(c) 日本の科学研究全般が急速に進展しているという状況。

(d) 日本の科学研究が失速寸前であるという状況。

【第2段落（前半）】

[2]

Since 2000, 17 Japanese have received Nobel Prizes in the natural sciences. But because most Nobel laureates receive the honor for what they accomplished 20 to 40 years earlier, such numbers do not necessarily reflect the nation's current scientific power. Conditions of Japan's scientific researchers have in fact deteriorated over the same period.

［**Words**］下記の語彙について、その意味を調べましょう。

	語彙	品詞	意味
1	laureate	名詞	
2	honor	名詞	
3	accomplish	動詞	
4	reflect	動詞	
5	current	形容詞	
6	condition	名詞	
7	researcher	名詞	
8	deteriorate	動詞	
9	period	名詞	

［**Phrases**］下記のフレーズについて、その意味を調べましょう。

	フレーズ	意味
1	Nobel Prizes	
2	the natural sciences	
3	a Nobel laureate	
4	20 to 40 years earlier	

5	not necessarily	
6	scientific power	
7	in fact	
8	over the same period	

［**Comprehension**］本文に即して、下記の問いに答えましょう。

1. 本文の内容と合致するものを、すべて選びましょう。

　　(a) 2000 年以降、医学の分野では、17 人の日本人がノーベル賞を受賞している。

　　(b) 日本のノーベル賞受賞者のほとんどは、ここ 10 年の間に成し遂げたことが評価されて、ノーベル賞を受賞している。

　　(c) 2000 年以降、日本の科学者が置かれている状況は、悪化してきている。

【第 2 段落（後半）】

The government's research and development spending has been flat since 2001 while other countries like China, South Korea and Germany have substantially increased their expenditures. In 2004, when the status of national universities was changed to one similar to independent administrative bodies, government grants to them began to fall, with the fiscal 2017 figure 10 percent less than in 2004.

［**Words**］下記の語彙について、その意味を調べましょう。

	語彙	品詞	意味
1	development	名詞	
2	spending	名詞	
3	flat	形容詞	
4	substantially	副詞	
5	increase	動詞	
6	expenditure	名詞	
7	status	名詞	
8	independent	形容詞	
9	fiscal	形容詞	
10	figure	名詞	

[**Phrases**] 下記のフレーズについて、その意味を調べましょう。

	フレーズ	意味
1	South Korea	
2	a national university	
3	(be) similar to ～	
4	independent administrative bodies	
5	government grants	

[**Comprehension**] 本文に即して、下記の問いに答えましょう。

1. 日本の科学研究の現状に関して、正しい記述となっているものを、下記から1つ選びましょう。

    (a) 研究開発に関わる日本政府の支出は、2000年以降、大幅に増加している。

    (b) 研究開発に関わる日本政府の支出は、2014年以降、横ばい状態が続いている。

    (c) 国立大学に交付される政府の補助金は、2004年以降、減少している。

    (d) 2017年に国立大学に交付された政府の補助金は、前年度に比べて、10％減少している。

Dictation

※音声を聞いて、語彙を書き取りましょう。

[1]　TRACK No. 24

In the 150 years since the Meiji Restoration, (^{1}) in science and technology has been one of the key driving forces behind Japan's modernization. Today, however, the overall prospect of the nation's (^{2}) research isn't all that promising. While rapid progress is being made in (^{3}) science and robotics, various data show that Japan's scientific research is on the verge of stalling. The government, universities and other research institutes must take the situation seriously and take (^{4}) steps to address the problem.

[2]　TRACK No. 25

Since 2000, 17 Japanese have (^{5}) Nobel Prizes in the natural sciences. But because most Nobel laureates receive the honor for what they accomplished 20 to

40 years earlier, such numbers do not necessarily (^{6}) the nation's current scientific power. Conditions of Japan's scientific (^{7}) have in fact deteriorated over the same period. The government's research and development spending has been (^{8}) since 2001 while other countries like China, South Korea and Germany have substantially increased their expenditures. In 2004, when the status of national universities was changed to one similar to (^{9}) administrative bodies, government grants to them began to fall, with the (^{10}) 2017 figure 10 percent less than in 2004.

【195 words—*The Japan Times* (JAN 9, 2018)】

[MEMO]

....

....

....

....

....

....

....

....

....

....

....

....

Useful Phrases

※下線部に留意しながら、下記の英文を和訳しましょう。

TRACK No. 26

1. The volume of the cone is 42.8 cubic centimeters.

2. Shake the test tube gently for a few seconds.

3. This principle was discovered in the early 20th century.

Vocabulary Building

※音声を聞いて、フレーズを完成させましょう。その上で、そのフレーズが意味しているものを線で結びましょう。

TRACK No. 27

1. a (   ) (   ) ・   ・ 線分
2. the (   ) (   ) ・   ・ 気候変動
3. a (   ) (   ) ・   ・ 十分条件
4. an (   ) (   ) ・   ・ 動物界
5. (   ) (   ) ・   ・ 細胞壁
6. a (   ) (   ) ・   ・ 情報科学
7. (   ) (   ) ・   ・ 産業用ロボット
8. (   ) (   ) ・   ・ 自然科学

Unit 7

Alcohol Dependency

Reading Passage

[1]

But alcohol can pose dangers even when one is not dependent on it. Drinking beyond reasonable levels raises the risk of acute alcoholic poisoning, lifestyle-induced illnesses, cancer, depression and other health problems. It also contributes to traffic accidents, workplace accidents, domestic violence and suicides. Alcohol abuse can also lead to joblessness and poverty.

[2]

A major problem in Japan, experts point out, is the lack of social recognition that alcohol dependency is an illness. In a society where drinking tends to be promoted as a virtue, addiction to alcohol is often misunderstood as a problem resulting from a person's weak character. This view, in turn, can help to discourage people from receiving appropriate treatment. While many alcoholics are middle-aged men, the ranks of elderly and women who suffer from alcoholism are growing. Studies show that women tend to develop alcohol-dependency symptoms much more quickly than men.

[3]

According to the WHO, the harmful use of alcohol kills 2.5 million people a year worldwide and is the third leading risk factor for poor health globally. The WHO strategy cites key areas for policy actions at the national level, including leadership, awareness and commitment, responses of health services and community action, and priority areas for global action, such as public-health advocacy, technical support and capacity building and production, and dissemination of knowledge.

【218 words—*The Japan Times* (JAN 27, 2014)】

[Note] WHO (World Health Organization)：世界保健機関

[1]

But alcohol can pose dangers even when one is not dependent on it. Drinking beyond reasonable levels raises the risk of acute alcoholic poisoning, lifestyle-induced illnesses, cancer, depression and other health problems. It also contributes to traffic accidents, workplace accidents, domestic violence and suicides. Alcohol abuse can also lead to joblessness and poverty.

［**Words**］下記の語彙について、その意味を調べましょう。

	語彙	品詞	意味
1	alcohol	名詞	
2	pose	動詞	
3	danger	名詞	
4	raise	動詞	
5	cancer	名詞	
6	depression	名詞	
7	suicide	名詞	
8	joblessness	名詞	
9	poverty	名詞	

［**Phrases**］下記のフレーズについて、その意味を調べましょう。

	フレーズ	意味
1	be not dependent on ~	
2	beyond reasonable levels	
3	acute alcoholic poisoning	
4	lifestyle-induced illnesses	
5	health problems	
6	contribute to ~	
7	traffic accidents	
8	workplace accidents	
9	domestic violence	
10	alcohol abuse	
11	lead to ~	

[**Comprehension**] 本文に即して、下記の問いに答えましょう。

1. アルコール依存が引き起こしうる影響として、第1段落で指摘されているものを、下記からすべて選びましょう。

    (a) うつ病　(b) 急性アルコール中毒　(c) 離婚　(d) 家庭内暴力　(e) がん

    (f) 交通事故　(g) 万引き　(h) 生活習慣病

【第2段落】　

[2]

A major problem in Japan, experts point out, is the lack of social recognition that alcohol dependency is an illness. In a society where drinking tends to be promoted as a virtue, addiction to alcohol is often misunderstood as a problem resulting from a person's weak character. This view, in turn, can help to discourage people from receiving appropriate treatment. While many alcoholics are middle-aged men, the ranks of elderly and women who suffer from alcoholism are growing. Studies show that women tend to develop alcohol-dependency symptoms much more quickly than men.

[**Words**] 下記の語彙について、その意味を調べましょう。

	語彙	品詞	意味
1	expert	名詞	
2	promote	動詞	
3	virtue	名詞	
4	addiction	名詞	
5	character	名詞	
6	view	名詞	
7	alcoholic	名詞	
8	rank	名詞	
9	elderly	名詞	
10	alcoholism	名詞	
11	develop	動詞	
12	symptom	名詞	

[**Phrases**] 下記のフレーズについて、その意味を調べましょう。

	フレーズ	意味
1	point out	
2	the lack of social recognition	
3	alcohol dependency	
4	tend to *do*	
5	be misunderstood as ~	
6	result from ~	
7	in turn	
8	help to *do*	
9	discourage X from *doing*	
10	receive appropriate treatment	
11	middle-aged men	
12	suffer from ~	
13	much more quickly	

[**Comprehension**] 本文に即して、下記の問いに答えましょう。

1. アルコール依存症患者が適切な治療を受けることをためらってしまっているのは、なぜですか。下記の空欄にふさわしい語句を入れましょう。

「日本では、飲酒が（ ① ）と考えられているため、アルコール依存症は（ ② ）ではなく、その人の（ ③ ）が原因であるとの見方が一般的であるから。」

①	
②	
③	

【第3段落】

[3]

According to the WHO, the harmful use of alcohol kills 2.5 million people a year worldwide and is the third leading risk factor for poor health globally. The WHO strategy cites key areas for policy actions at the national level, including leadership, awareness and commitment, responses of health services and community action, and priority areas for global action, such as public-health advocacy, technical support and capacity building and production, and dissemination of knowledge.

[**Words**] 下記の語彙について、その意味を調べましょう。

	語彙	品詞	意味
1	harmful	形容詞	
2	worldwide	副詞	
3	leading	形容詞	
4	globally	副詞	
5	strategy	名詞	
6	cite	動詞	
7	leadership	名詞	
8	awareness	名詞	
9	commitment	名詞	
10	response	名詞	
11	dissemination	名詞	

[**Phrases**] 下記のフレーズについて、その意味を調べましょう。

	フレーズ	意味
1	according to ~	
2	2.5 million people	
3	a risk factor	
4	poor health	
5	policy actions	
6	at the national level	
7	health services	
8	community action	
9	priority areas	
10	public-health advocacy	
11	technical support	
12	capacity building and production	

[**Comprehension**] 本文に即して、下記の問いに答えましょう。

1. WHO が推進しているアルコール依存症対策に含まれないと考えられるもの
   は、次のうち、どれですか。1つ選びましょう。

   (a) アルコール依存症に関する正確な知識を普及させること。

   (b) 国がアルコール依存症対策を主導すること。

   (c) 地方自治体がアルコールの流通量を制限すること。

   (d) 世界規模で公衆衛生を保護すること。

Dictation

※音声を聞いて、語彙を書き取りましょう。

[1]

TRACK No. 28

But alcohol can pose dangers even when one is not (^{1}) on it. Drinking beyond reasonable levels raises the (^{2}) of acute alcoholic poisoning, lifestyle-induced illnesses, cancer, depression and other health problems. It also contributes to traffic accidents, workplace accidents, domestic violence and (^{3}). Alcohol abuse can also lead to joblessness and poverty.

[2]

TRACK No. 29

A major problem in Japan, experts point out, is the lack of social recognition that alcohol dependency is an (^{4}). In a society where drinking tends to be promoted as a virtue, addiction to alcohol is often (^{5}) as a problem resulting from a person's weak character. This view, in turn, can help to discourage people from receiving (^{6}) treatment. While many alcoholics are middle-aged men, the ranks of elderly and women who suffer from alcoholism are growing. Studies show that women tend to develop alcohol-dependency (^{7}) much more quickly than men.

[3]

TRACK No. 30

According to the WHO, the harmful use of alcohol kills 2.5 million people a year worldwide and is the third leading risk (^{8}) for poor health globally. The WHO strategy cites key areas for policy actions at the national level, including leadership, awareness and commitment, (^{9}) of health services and community action, and priority areas for global action, such as public-health advocacy, technical support and (^{10}) building and production, and dissemination of knowledge.

【218 words—*The Japan Times* (JAN 27, 2014)】

[MEMO]

....

....

....

Useful Phrases

※下線部に留意しながら、下記の英文を和訳しましょう。

TRACK No. 31

1. In the latter case, air friction is negligible.

2. This equation has at least two solutions.

3. In Table 5, the total number of subjects is shown in italics.

Vocabulary Building

※音声を聞いて、フレーズを完成させましょう。その上で、そのフレーズが意味しているものを線で結びましょう。

TRACK No. 32

1.　　　　　　　a (　　　　　) (　　　　) ・　・ 自然淘汰
2.　　　　　the (　　　　　) (　　　　) ・　・ 単細胞生物
3. a (　　　　)-(　　　　) (　　　　) ・　・ 空気抵抗
4.　　　　　　　(　　　　　) (　　　　) ・　・ バイオテクノロジー
5.　　　　　　　(　　　　　) (　　　　) ・　・ 自然環境
6.　　　　　　　　　　　 (　　　　) ・　・ 化学反応
7.　　　　　　an (　　　　　) (　　　　) ・　・ ハイブリッド車
8.　　　　　　 a (　　　　　) (　　　　) ・　・ 虫刺され

Agricultural Products

Reading Passage

[1]

Attention should be paid to the fact that Japan's agricultural products such as fruits and vegetables are of high quality. If farmers are keen to the needs of consumers and able to supply agricultural products wanted by consumers in a consistent manner, they can expect to increase their profits. These days many consumers want agricultural products that are organically produced and are chemical free.

[2]

Japan's agriculture finds itself in a difficult situation. The number of farmers is on the decline as their average age increases. If Japan takes part in the Transpacific Partnership free trade zone, they will be exposed to harsh competition. But as more manufacturers move their production bases to foreign countries and the employment situation in local economies becomes difficult, agriculture can play an important role in creating jobs.

[3]

The government needs to seriously consider ways to revitalize the agricultural sector and farming communities so that they can ensure sufficient incomes for workers, thus making agriculture more attractive to people who are looking for jobs.

[4]

If farmers can expand their activities to include processing of agricultural products as well as the distribution and sale of agricultural products, they can diversify the sources of their income as well as increase their incomes. Such activities will also shorten the psychological distance between agricultural producers and consumers. It will be important for farmers to push product differentiation and to acquire the know-how needed for marketing and running a business.

【239 words—*The Japan Times* (MAY 31, 2012)】

[Note] Transpacific Partnership：環太平洋経済連携協定

[1]

Attention should be paid to the fact that Japan's agricultural products such as fruits and vegetables are of high quality. If farmers are keen to the needs of consumers and able to supply agricultural products wanted by consumers in a consistent manner, they can expect to increase their profits. These days many consumers want agricultural products that are organically produced and are chemical free.

［**Words**］下記の語彙について、その意味を調べましょう。

	語彙	品詞	意味
1	farmer	名詞	
2	consumer	名詞	
3	supply	動詞	
4	profit	名詞	

［**Phrases**］下記のフレーズについて、その意味を調べましょう。

	フレーズ	意味
1	pay attention to ~	
2	agricultural products	
3	be of high quality	
4	be keen to ~	
5	in a consistent manner	
6	expect to *do*	
7	these days	
8	be organically produced	
9	be chemical free	

［**Comprehension**］本文に即して、下記の問いに答えましょう。

1. 農業従事者が利益の増加を期待できると考えられるのは、次のうち、どれですか。1つ選びましょう。

    (a) 有機栽培された農作物や農薬不使用の農作物を提供する。

    (b) 長く日持ちのするように品種改良された農作物を提供する。

    (c) 流通経路を見直すことで、より新鮮な農作物を提供する。

    (d) 農薬を使用しても、品質の高い農作物を提供する。

[2]

Japan's agriculture finds itself in a difficult situation. The number of farmers is on the decline as their average age increases. If Japan takes part in the Transpacific Partnership free trade zone, they will be exposed to harsh competition. But as more manufacturers move their production bases to foreign countries and the employment situation in local economies becomes difficult, agriculture can play an important role in creating jobs.

［**Words**］ 下記の語彙について、その意味を調べましょう。

	語彙	品詞	意味
1	agriculture	名詞	
2	situation	名詞	
3	average	形容詞	
4	transpacific	形容詞	
5	manufacturer	名詞	
6	employment	名詞	

［**Phrases**］ 下記のフレーズについて、その意味を調べましょう。

	フレーズ	意味
1	the number of ~	
2	be on the decline	
3	take part in ~	
4	a free trade zone	
5	be exposed to ~	
6	harsh competition	
7	production bases	
8	local economies	
9	become difficult	
10	play an important role in ~	

［**Comprehension**］ 本文に即して、下記の問いに答えましょう。

1. 本文中の "a difficult situation" とは、具体的にどのような状況のことを指していますか。正しい答えを、下記からすべて選びましょう。

    (a) 高齢化にともなって、農業従事者の数が減少傾向にあること。

    (b) 度重なる異常気象のせいで、農作物の不作が続いていること。

(c) TPP 自由貿易圏への参加によって、より厳しい競争にさらされるかも
しれないこと。

(d) 農業に対する魅力が少ないため、若者の農業離れが進んでいること。

(e) 生産基地を外国に移転しているため、地域経済の雇用状況が厳しくなっ
ていること。

【第3段落】

[3]

The government needs to seriously consider ways to revitalize the agricultural sector and farming communities so that they can ensure sufficient incomes for workers, thus making agriculture more attractive to people who are looking for jobs.

［**Words**］下記の語彙について、その意味を調べましょう。

	語彙	品詞	意味
1	government	名詞	
2	seriously	副詞	
3	consider	動詞	
4	revitalize	動詞	
5	ensure	動詞	
6	thus	接続詞	
7	attractive	形容詞	

［**Phrases**］下記のフレーズについて、その意味を調べましょう。

	フレーズ	意味
1	the agricultural sector	
2	farming communities	
3	sufficient incomes	
4	look for jobs	

［**Comprehension**］本文に即して、下記の問いに答えましょう。

1. 現状を打破するために、日本政府はどのような対策を取ることができますか。
下記の空欄にふさわしい語句を入れましょう。

「労働者に（ ① ）を保証できるように、農業部門や農業コミュニティー

を（②）させる方法を真剣に検討するとともに、仕事を探している人に
とって農業をより（③）なものにしていくという対策。」

	①	
	②	
	③	

【第4段落】

[4]

If farmers can expand their activities to include processing of agricultural products as well as the distribution and sale of agricultural products, they can diversify the sources of their income as well as increase their incomes. Such activities will also shorten the psychological distance between agricultural producers and consumers. It will be important for farmers to push product differentiation and to acquire the know-how needed for marketing and running a business.

［**Words**］ 下記の語彙について、その意味を調べましょう。

	語彙	品詞	意味
1	expand	動詞	
2	processing	名詞	
3	distribution	名詞	
4	sale	名詞	
5	diversify	動詞	
6	income	名詞	
7	shorten	動詞	
8	push	動詞	
9	acquire	動詞	
10	know-how	名詞	
11	marketing	名詞	

［**Phrases**］ 下記のフレーズについて、その意味を調べましょう。

	フレーズ	意味
1	a psychological distance	
2	agricultural producers	
3	product differentiation	
4	run a business	

［**Comprehension**］本文に即して、下記の問いに答えましょう。

1. 現状を打破するために、農業従事者はどのような対策を取ることができますか。第4段落で指摘されているものを、下記からすべて選びましょう。

    (a) 農作物の流通と販売に加えて、農作物の加工も行うなどして収入源を多様化させること。

    (b) インターネット上での農作物の販売に力を注ぐことで、生産者と消費者の間の心理的距離を縮めること。

    (c) あくまでも効率的な農作物の生産に注力し、経営は民間企業に委託すること。

    (d) マーケティングやビジネス経営のために必要とされるノウハウを、農業従事者が習得すること。

［MEMO］

....

....

....

....

....

Dictation

※音声を聞いて、語彙を書き取りましょう。

[1]

TRACK No. 33

Attention should be paid to the (^{1}) that Japan's agricultural products such as fruits and vegetables are of high quality. If farmers are keen (^{2}) the needs of consumers and able to supply agricultural products wanted by consumers in a consistent manner, they can expect to increase their (^{3}). These days many consumers want agricultural products that are organically produced and are chemical free.

[2]

TRACK No. 34

Japan's agriculture finds (^{4}) in a difficult situation. The number of farmers is on the decline as their average age increases. If Japan takes part (^{5}) the Transpacific Partnership free trade zone, they will be exposed to harsh competition. But as more manufacturers move their production bases to foreign countries and the employment situation in local economies becomes difficult, agriculture can play an important (^{6}) in creating jobs.

[3]

TRACK No. 35

The government needs to seriously consider ways to revitalize the agricultural sector and farming communities so that they can ensure sufficient incomes for workers, thus making agriculture more (^{7}) to people who are looking for jobs.

[4]

TRACK No. 36

If farmers can expand their activities to include processing of agricultural products as well as the distribution and sale of agricultural products, they can diversify the (^{8}) of their income as well as increase their incomes. Such activities will also shorten the psychological distance (^{9}) agricultural producers and consumers. It will be important for farmers to push product differentiation and to (^{10}) the know-how needed for marketing and running a business.

【239 words—*The Japan Times* (MAY 31, 2012)】

Useful Phrases

※下線部に留意しながら、下記の英文を和訳しましょう。

TRACK No. 37

1. This kind of criticism <u>would be obviously pointless</u>.

2. <u>The length of the diagonal</u> is about 9.5 centimeters.

3. In general, electrons <u>have a negative charge</u>.

Vocabulary Building

※音声を聞いて、フレーズを完成させましょう。その上で、そのフレーズが意味しているものを線で結びましょう。

TRACK No. 38

1. a (   ) (   ) ・   ・ コンピュータウイルス
2.   (   ) (   ) ・   ・ 外来種
3. a (   ) (   ) ・   ・ 自然災害
4.   (   ) (   ) ・   ・ 人工知能
5. an (   ) (   ) ・   ・ 幹細胞
6.   (   ) (   ) ・   ・ 環境問題
7. a (   ) (   ) ・   ・ 食中毒
8.   (   ) (   ) ・   ・ 花粉症

Unit 9

Organ Transplants

Reading Passage

[1]

Under the original law, removal of organs from brain-dead patients was only possible if the patients had expressed in writing in advance their willingness to donate their organs and their family members approved the transplant. This requirement automatically excluded donors under 15 since the Civil Code does not recognize wills written by people below that age.

[2]

However, an amendment that took effect in 2010 has made it possible to harvest organs from patients who had not expressed their readiness to donate. Unless patients had clearly indicated their refusal to have their organs removed, transplants can be carried out with the approval of their relatives. Following the revision, the number of organ donations from brain-dead patients increased from about 10 cases a year to around 60. Last year saw a record 64 donation cases, including 51 that involved a heart transplant.

[3]

The amendment also paved the way for organ transplants from small children. For example, a boy less than 6 years old was judged to be in a state of brain death in a hospital in Hiroshima Prefecture in May and his lungs were transplanted to a 1-year-old girl at Okayama University Hospital and his heart to a boy under 10 at University of Tokyo Hospital.

【263 words—*The Japan Times* (OCT 7, 2017)】

[1]

Under the original law, removal of organs from brain-dead patients was only possible if the patients had expressed in writing in advance their willingness to donate their organs and their family members approved the transplant. This requirement automatically excluded donors under 15 since the Civil Code does not recognize wills written by people below that age.

[Note] the original law：この場合は、1997 年 10 月 16 日に施行された「臓器移植法」を指す。

[**Words**] 下記の語彙について、その意味を調べましょう。

	語彙	品詞	意味
1	removal	名詞	
2	organ	名詞	
3	express	動詞	
4	willingness	名詞	
5	donate	動詞	
6	approve	動詞	
7	transplant	名詞	
8	requirement	名詞	
9	automatically	副詞	
10	exclude	動詞	
11	donor	名詞	
12	recognize	動詞	
13	will	名詞	

[**Phrases**] 下記のフレーズについて、その意味を調べましょう。

	フレーズ	意味
1	under the original law	
2	brain-dead patients	
3	in advance	
4	family members	
5	donors under 15	
6	the Civil Code	
7	people below that age	

［**Comprehension**］本文に即して、下記の問いに答えましょう。

1. 本文1行目に登場する "the original law"（臓器移植法）の下で、脳死後の臓器
   提供が可能となるケースは、下記のA～Dのうち、どれですか。ふさわしいも
   のをすべて選びましょう。

	A	B	C	D
脳死患者の年齢	12歳	18歳	30歳	80歳
書面による臓器提供の意思表示	あり	なし	あり	あり
家族の同意	あり	あり	あり	なし

【**第2段落**】

[2]

However, an amendment that took effect in 2010 has made it possible to harvest organs from patients who had not expressed their readiness to donate. Unless patients had clearly indicated their refusal to have their organs removed, transplants can be carried out with the approval of their relatives. Following the revision, the number of organ donations from brain-dead patients increased from about 10 cases a year to around 60. Last year saw a record 64 donation cases, including 51 that involved a heart transplant.

［**Words**］下記の語彙について、その意味を調べましょう。

	語彙	品詞	意味
1	amendment	名詞	
2	harvest	動詞	
3	readiness	名詞	
4	unless	接続詞	
5	clearly	副詞	
6	indicate	動詞	
7	refusal	名詞	
8	remove	動詞	
9	relative	名詞	
10	following	前置詞	
11	revision	名詞	
12	donation	名詞	
13	record	形容詞	
14	involve	動詞	

	フレーズ	意味
1	take effect	
2	make it possible to *do*	
3	carry out	
4	with the approval of ~	
5	the number of organ donations	
6	about 10 cases a year	
7	around 60	
8	a heart transplant	

[**Comprehension**] 本文に即して、下記の問いに答えましょう。

1. 本文の内容と合致するものを、すべて選びましょう。

(a) 2010 年に改正臓器移植法が施行されたことによって、脳死患者の親族から承認が得られない場合でも、臓器を摘出することが可能になった。

(b) 2010 年に改正臓器移植法が施行されたことによって、臓器提供の意思を事前に書面で表明していなかった患者からも、臓器を摘出することが可能になった。

(c) 2010 年に改正臓器移植法が施行されると、脳死患者からの臓器提供件数は、改正前のおよそ 6 倍にまで増加した。

(d) 2016 年には 64 件の臓器提供が行われたが、そのうちの 51 件は腎臓移植に関わるものであった。

【第 3 段落】

[3]

The amendment also paved the way for organ transplants from small children. For example, a boy less than 6 years old was judged to be in a state of brain death in a hospital in Hiroshima Prefecture in May and his lungs were transplanted to a 1-year-old girl at Okayama University Hospital and his heart to a boy under 10 at University of Tokyo Hospital.

［**Words**］下記の語彙について、その意味を調べましょう。

	語彙	品詞	意味
1	prefecture	名詞	
2	lung	名詞	
3	transplant	動詞	

［**Phrases**］下記のフレーズについて、その意味を調べましょう。

	フレーズ	意味
1	pave the way for ~	
2	organ transplants	
3	a boy less than 6 years old	
4	be judged to *do*	
5	be in a state of ~	
6	brain death	
7	a 1-year-old girl	
8	Okayama University Hospital	
9	a boy under 10	
10	University of Tokyo Hospital	

［**Comprehension**］本文に即して、下記の問いに答えましょう。

1. 本文の内容に合わせて、空欄を埋めましょう。

- （①）県の病院で、5月に、男児（6歳未満）が脳死状態と判定された。
- その後、その男児の（②）は、（③）に入院中の女児（1歳）に移植された。
- また、その男児の（④）は、（⑤）に入院中の男児（10歳未満）に移植された。

①	
②	
③	
④	
⑤	

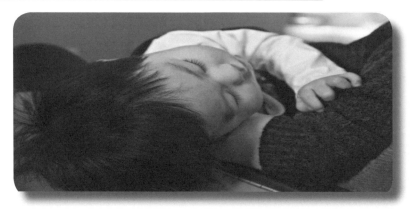

Dictation

※音声を聞いて、語彙を書き取りましょう。

[1]

TRACK No. 39

Under the original law, removal of (^{1}) from brain-dead patients was only possible if the patients had (^{2}) in writing in advance their willingness to donate their organs and their family members approved the transplant. This requirement automatically (^{3}) donors under 15 since the Civil Code does not recognize wills written by people below that age.

[2]

TRACK No. 40

However, an amendment that took effect in 2010 has made it possible to (^{4}) organs from patients who had not expressed their readiness to donate. Unless patients had clearly (^{5}) their refusal to have their organs removed, transplants can be carried out with the approval of their relatives. (^{6}) the revision, the number of organ donations from brain-dead patients (^{7}) from about 10 cases a year to around 60. Last year saw a record 64 donation cases, including 51 that involved a (^{8}) transplant.

[3]

TRACK No. 41

The amendment also paved the way for organ transplants from small children. For example, a boy less than 6 years old was judged to be in a (^{9}) of brain death in a hospital in Hiroshima Prefecture in May and his (^{10}) were transplanted to a 1-year-old girl at Okayama University Hospital and his heart to a boy under 10 at University of Tokyo Hospital.

【263 words—*The Japan Times* (OCT 7, 2017)】

[MEMO]

....

....

....

Useful Phrases

※下線部に留意しながら、下記の英文を和訳しましょう。

TRACK No. 42

1. These reagents should be stored at normal temperature.

2. The slope of this straight line is 3.

3. This hypothesis must be tested experimentally.

Vocabulary Building

※音声を聞いて、フレーズを完成させましょう。その上で、そのフレーズが意味しているものを線で結びましょう。

TRACK No. 43

1.	a (　　　) (　　　) ・	・ 臨床試験
2.	the (　　　) (　　　) (　　　) ・	・ 酸性雨
3.	(　　　) (　　　) ・	・ 二酸化炭素
4.	(　　　) (　　　) ・	・ 原子爆弾
5.	(　　　) (　　　) ・	・ 進化生物学
6.	(　　　) (　　　) ・	・ スペースシャトル
7.	an (　　　) (　　　) ・	・ 細胞分裂
8.	a (　　　) (　　　) ・	・ 全地球測位 システム（GPS）

Unit 10

Extreme Weather

Reading Passage

[1]

Heat is not the only manifestation of extreme weather. Japan has experienced some of the worst damage from torrential rainfall in recent history, with more than 200 people dead or unaccounted for in the downpours that caused flooding and landslides in broad areas of western Japan in early July. Climate scientists attribute the flooding and heavy rains of recent years to climate change since warmer air holds more warm water, which results in more intense rainfall.

[2]

While weather is a local phenomenon, it reflects long-term climate trends. In other words, extreme weather is the evidence of climate change. Scientists warn that this summer's heat wave will soon become ordinary. The question is what we can do to reduce the damage, both now and in the future. Governments must get serious about greenhouse gas reductions to slow the changes already underway. The 2015 Paris climate accord is a start, but it is only that.

[3]

Equally important are efforts to mitigate the harm, which in an aging society requires far more systemic and creative solutions. Japan has to rethink fundamental assumptions about energy use and urban planning. It is a daunting assignment, but one in which this country can excel and lead the world.

【202 words—*The Japan Times* (JUL 30, 2018)】

[1]

Heat is not the only manifestation of extreme weather. Japan has experienced some of the worst damage from torrential rainfall in recent history, with more than 200 people dead or unaccounted for in the downpours that caused flooding and landslides in broad areas of western Japan in early July. Climate scientists attribute the flooding and heavy rains of recent years to climate change since warmer air holds more warm water, which results in more intense rainfall.

[**Words**] 下記の語彙について、その意味を調べましょう。

	語彙	品詞	意味
1	manifestation	名詞	
2	experience	動詞	
3	downpour	名詞	
4	cause	動詞	
5	flooding	名詞	
6	landslide	名詞	
7	intense	形容詞	
8	rainfall	名詞	

[**Phrases**] 下記のフレーズについて、その意味を調べましょう。

	フレーズ	意味
1	extreme weather	
2	torrential rainfall	
3	be unaccounted for	
4	in broad areas of western Japan	
5	in early July	
6	climate scientists	
7	attribute X to Y	
8	heavy rains	
9	climate change	
10	result in ~	

[**Comprehension**] 本文に即して、下記の問いに答えましょう。

1. 異常気象の表れには、「暑さ」以外に何があると、本文には書かれていますか。

[2]

While weather is a local phenomenon, it reflects long-term climate trends. In other words, extreme weather is the evidence of climate change. Scientists warn that this summer's heat wave will soon become ordinary. The question is what we can do to reduce the damage, both now and in the future. Governments must get serious about greenhouse gas reductions to slow the changes already underway. The 2015 Paris climate accord is a start, but it is only that.

[**Words**] 下記の語彙について、その意味を調べましょう。

	語彙	品詞	意味
1	reflect	動詞	
2	long-term	形容詞	
3	evidence	名詞	
4	warn	動詞	
5	reduce	動詞	
6	accord	名詞	

[**Phrases**] 下記のフレーズについて、その意味を調べましょう。

	フレーズ	意味
1	a local phenomenon	
2	climate trends	
3	in other words	
4	this summer's heat wave	
5	become ordinary	
6	in the future	
7	get serious about ~	

8	greenhouse gas reductions	
9	be already underway	

［**Comprehension**］本文に即して、下記の問いに答えましょう。

1. 進行中の気候変動を抑制するために、各国政府に求められていることとは、
   どのようなことですか。1つ選んで記号で答えましょう。

　　　(a) 森林を保全し、管理すること。

　　　(b) 温室効果ガスを削減すること。

　　　(c) 水資源を適切に管理すること。

　　　(d) より正確な気候変動予測を行うこと。

【第3段落】

[3]

Equally important are efforts to mitigate the harm, which in an aging society requires
far more systemic and creative solutions. Japan has to rethink fundamental assumptions
about energy use and urban planning. It is a daunting assignment, but one in which this
country can excel and lead the world.

［**Words**］下記の語彙について、その意味を調べましょう。

	語彙	品詞	意味
1	equally	副詞	
2	effort	名詞	
3	mitigate	動詞	
4	harm	名詞	
5	systemic	形容詞	
6	creative	形容詞	
7	solution	名詞	
8	rethink	動詞	
9	daunting	形容詞	
10	assignment	名詞	
11	excel	動詞	
12	lead	動詞	

	フレーズ	意味
1	an aging society	
2	fundamental assumptions	
3	energy use	
4	urban planning	

[**Comprehension**]　本文に即して、下記の問いに答えましょう。

1. 気候変動による被害を最小限に抑えるために、日本が行わなければならない
   こととは、次のうちどれですか。1つ選んで記号で答えましょう。

    (a) 少子化対策と高齢者福祉に関する基本事項の再考。

    (b) エネルギー使用と都市計画に関する基本事項の再考。

    (c) エネルギー政策と税制に関する基本事項の再考。

    (d) 福祉政策とエネルギー政策に関する基本事項の再考。

Dictation

※音声を聞いて、語彙を書き取りましょう。

[1]

TRACK No. 44

Heat is not the (^{1}) manifestation of extreme weather. Japan has experienced some of the (^{2}) damage from torrential rainfall in recent history, with more than 200 people dead or unaccounted for in the downpours that (^{3}) flooding and landslides in broad areas of western Japan in early July. Climate scientists attribute the flooding and heavy rains of recent years to climate change since warmer air holds more warm water, which results (^{4}) more intense rainfall.

[2]

TRACK No. 45

(^{5}) weather is a local phenomenon, it reflects long-term climate trends. In other words, extreme weather is the evidence of climate change. Scientists warn that this summer's heat wave will soon become (^{6}). The question is what we can do to reduce the damage, both now and in the future. Governments must get serious (^{7}) greenhouse gas reductions to slow the changes already underway. The 2015 Paris climate accord is a (^{8}), but it is only that.

[3]

TRACK No. 46

Equally important are efforts to mitigate the harm, which in an aging society requires (^{9}) more systemic and creative solutions. Japan has to rethink fundamental assumptions about energy use and urban planning. It is a daunting assignment, but one in which this country can excel and (^{10}) the world.

【202 words—*The Japan Times* (JUL 30, 2018)】

[MEMO]

···

···

···

···

Useful Phrases

※下線部に留意しながら、下記の英文を和訳しましょう。

TRACK No. 47

1. In Figure 2, this relationship is represented by a dotted line.

2. This is known as the law of conservation of mass.

3. Add the solution drop by drop.

Vocabulary Building

※音声を聞いて、フレーズを完成させましょう。その上で、そのフレーズが意味しているものを線で結びましょう。

TRACK No. 48

1. ( ) ( ) ・	・ 地下水
2. a ( ) ( ) ・	・ 遺伝子治療
3. ( ) ( ) ・	・ 酸素原子
4. ( ) ( ) ・	・ 核兵器
5. an ( ) ( ) ・	・ 植物生態学
6. ( ) ( ) ・	・ 宇宙科学
7. ( ) ・	・ 化石燃料
8. a ( ) ( ) ・	・ 土壌汚染

Unit 11

Wild Animals

Reading Passage

[1]

The rapidly expanding deer and wild boar population in Japan is having a serious impact on the nation's agriculture and ecosystems. The population of deer was estimated at 3.25 million and that of wild boars at 880,000 across the country as of 2011. The government has proposed an amendment to the law on animal protection, calling for efforts to reduce the number of wild animals to appropriate levels. The challenge is how to secure the manpower and other resources to meet the targets.

[2]

The deer population has sharply increased as many of the nation's aging hunters have retired. The government also believes that their habitat has expanded as a widening area of Japan's farmland has been abandoned with the decline in the number of farmers and that changes in ecosystems due to global warming has reduced the number of deer that die of starvation in winter.

[3]

These animals' growing numbers have caused severe damage to agricultural production, which is estimated to reach ¥20 billion annually. Signs of the impact on ecosystems have also been found in many of Japan's national parks, where trees have withered after their bark was eaten by deer, alpine plants have been consumed and mudslides have taken place in areas where vegetation has been stripped away by foraging animals. To prevent further damage, these animal populations need to be controlled.

【224 words—*The Japan Times* (MAY 1, 2014)】

78

[1]

The rapidly expanding deer and wild boar population in Japan is having a serious impact on the nation's agriculture and ecosystems. The population of deer was estimated at 3.25 million and that of wild boars at 880,000 across the country as of 2011. The government has proposed an amendment to the law on animal protection, calling for efforts to reduce the number of wild animals to appropriate levels. The challenge is how to secure the manpower and other resources to meet the targets.

[**Words**] 下記の語彙について、その意味を調べましょう。

		語彙	品詞	意味
	1	rapidly	副詞	
	2	expand	動詞	
	3	deer	名詞	
	4	population	名詞	
	5	agriculture	名詞	
	6	ecosystem	名詞	
	7	propose	動詞	
	8	amendment	名詞	
	9	effort	名詞	
	10	reduce	動詞	
	11	appropriate	形容詞	
	12	challenge	名詞	
	13	secure	動詞	
	14	manpower	名詞	
	15	resource	名詞	

[**Phrases**] 下記のフレーズについて、その意味を調べましょう。

		フレーズ	意味
	1	a wild boar	
	2	have a serious impact on ~	
	3	the population of deer	
	4	be estimated at ~	
	5	3.25 million	
	6	across the country	
	7	as of 2011	

8	the law on animal protection	
9	call for ~	
10	the number of wild animals	
11	meet the targets	

[**Comprehension**] 本文に即して、下記の問いに答えましょう。

1. 本文の内容に合わせて、空欄を埋めましょう。

　　近年、日本において、シカやイノシシの個体数が（　①　）しており、日本の（　②　）や（　③　）に深刻な影響を与えている。政府は、（　④　）に関する法律の修正案を提案するなどの対策をとってはいるが、依然として多くの課題が残されている。

①	
②	
③	
④	

2. 6行目に登場する "the targets" は、何を指していますか。下記から1つ選びましょう。

　　(a) 激減しているシカやイノシシの個体数を、適切なレベルにまで増やすこと。

　　(b) 急増しているシカやイノシシの個体数を、適切なレベルにまで減らすこと。

　　(c) 動物保護に関する法律を改正すること。

　　(d) 増えすぎたシカやイノシシを間引くために、人材を確保すること。

【第2段落】

[2]

The deer population has sharply increased as many of the nation's aging hunters have retired. The government also believes that their habitat has expanded as a widening area of Japan's farmland has been abandoned with the decline in the number of farmers and that changes in ecosystems due to global warming has reduced the number of deer that die of starvation in winter.

[**Words**] 下記の語彙について、その意味を調べましょう。

	語彙	品詞	意味
1	sharply	副詞	
2	increase	動詞	
3	aging	形容詞	
4	hunter	名詞	
5	retire	動詞	
6	government	名詞	
7	habitat	名詞	
8	widen	動詞	
9	farmland	名詞	
10	abandon	動詞	
11	farmer	名詞	
12	starvation	名詞	

[**Phrases**] 下記のフレーズについて、その意味を調べましょう。

	フレーズ	意味
1	the decline in ~	
2	the number of farmers	
3	changes in ecosystems	
4	due to ~	
5	global warming	
6	die of starvation	

[**Comprehension**] 本文に即して、下記の問いに答えましょう。

1. シカの個体数が増加した理由として、本文に述べられているものを、下記からすべて選びましょう。

   (a) 高齢となった猟師の多くが引退しているから。

   (b) 農業従事者の数が減少するにつれて、農地が放棄されているから。

   (c) 森林破壊の結果、シカが本来の生息地から追い出されているから。

   (d) 空気汚染により、生態系に変化が生じているから。

   (e) 地球温暖化により、生態系に変化が生じているから。

［MEMO]

....

....

....

[3]

These animals' growing numbers have caused severe damage to agricultural production, which is estimated to reach ¥20 billion annually. Signs of the impact on ecosystems have also been found in many of Japan's national parks, where trees have withered after their bark was eaten by deer, alpine plants have been consumed and mudslides have taken place in areas where vegetation has been stripped away by foraging animals. To prevent further damage, these animal populations need to be controlled.

[**Words**] 下記の語彙について、その意味を調べましょう。

	語彙	品詞	意味
1	growing	形容詞	
2	cause	動詞	
3	agricultural	形容詞	
4	sign	名詞	
5	wither	動詞	
6	bark	名詞	
7	alpine	形容詞	
8	consume	動詞	
9	mudslide	名詞	
10	vegetation	名詞	
11	forage	動詞	
12	prevent	動詞	
13	further	形容詞	
14	control	動詞	

[**Phrases**] 下記のフレーズについて、その意味を調べましょう。

	フレーズ	意味
1	severe damage	
2	agricultural production	
3	be estimated to *do*	
4	reach ¥20 billion annually	
5	the impact on ecosystems	
6	national parks	
7	alpine plants	
8	take place	

9	be stripped away	
10	foraging animals	

[**Comprehension**] 本文に即して、下記の問いに答えましょう。

1. 2行目に登場する "Signs of the impact on ecosystems" とは、具体的にはどのような現象のことを意味していますか。下記からすべて選びましょう。

    (a) シカにより木の実が食い尽くされることで、木々が枯れてしまっていること。

    (b) 高山植物がシカによって食べられてしまっていること。

    (c) シカなどの動物によって草木が剥ぎ取られた地域で、泥流が起こっていること。

    (d) シカなどの害獣が農業生産に深刻な被害をもたらしており、損害額は年間で推定20億円に到達していること。

2. 急増しているシカへの対策に関して、本文の内容と合致するものを、下記から1つ選びましょう。

    (a) シカも生態系の一部であり、安易に殺すべきではない。

    (b) 国立公園でシカ専用のエリアを設け、保護すべきである。

    (c) 生態系への悪影響を深刻に受け止め、適切な個体数になるようにコントロールすべきである。

    (d) 間引いたシカは食肉として加工するなど、無駄に殺すことは避けるべきである。

Dictation

※音声を聞いて、語彙を書き取りましょう。

[1]

TRACK No. 49

The rapidly expanding deer and wild boar population in Japan is having a serious impact on the nation's (¹   ) and ecosystems. The population of deer was estimated at 3.25 million and that of wild boars at 880,000 across the country as of 2011. The government has proposed an amendment to the law on animal (²   ), calling for efforts to reduce the number of wild animals to appropriate levels. The challenge is how to secure the manpower and other (³   ) to meet the targets.

[2]

TRACK No. 50

The deer population has sharply increased as many of the nation's aging hunters have retired. The government also believes that their (⁴   ) has expanded as a widening area of Japan's (⁵   ) has been abandoned with the decline in the number of farmers and that changes in (⁶   ) due to global warming has reduced the number of deer that die of starvation in winter.

[3]

TRACK No. 51

These animals' growing numbers have (⁷   ) severe damage to agricultural production, which is estimated to reach ¥20 (⁸   ) annually. Signs of the impact on ecosystems have also been found in many of Japan's national parks, where trees have withered after their bark was eaten by deer, alpine plants have been (⁹   ) and mudslides have taken place in areas where vegetation has been stripped away by foraging animals. To prevent further damage, these animal populations need to be (¹⁰   ).

【224 words—*The Japan Times* (MAY 1, 2014)】

[MEMO]

……………………………………………………………………………………

……………………………………………………………………………………

……………………………………………………………………………………

Useful Phrases

※下線部に留意しながら、下記の英文を和訳しましょう。

TRACK No. 52

1. These aqueous solutions <u>are strongly basic</u>.

2. However, this explanation has been criticized <u>for three reasons</u>.

3. <u>The mass of this object</u> is 7.5 kilograms.

Vocabulary Building

※音声を聞いて、フレーズを完成させましょう。その上で、そのフレーズが意味しているものを線で結びましょう。

TRACK No.53

1. ( ) ( )	·	·	人工衛星
2. the ( ) ( )	·	·	大学院生
3. the ( ) ( ) ( )	·	·	地球科学
4. ( ) ( )	·	·	中枢神経系
5. a ( ) ( )	·	·	アミノ酸
6. a ( ) ( )	·	·	分子遺伝学
7. an ( ) ( )	·	·	消火器
8. ( ) ( )	·	·	太陽系

Unit 12
◇◇◇◇◇◇◇◇

Renewable Energy

Reading Passage

[1]

Google (or more accurately its parent company, Alphabet) is the world's second-largest corporation by market capitalization: It is worth more than $530 billion. Headquartered in the United States, it has a digital and physical footprint that stretches around the world; in addition to office complexes that house staff and scientists, the company has huge data farms dotted across the globe. Those farms house massive computing facilities that consume extraordinary amounts of energy. It is reckoned that Google consumed 5.2 terawatts of energy in 2015 — the equivalent of the energy needs of the city of San Francisco or half a million homes in the U.S.

[2]

In a bold move, Google announced in 2012 that it was committed to 100 percent renewable energy purchasing in its operations. This month it confirmed that it will by 2017 purchase enough green energy to meet all its energy needs. Currently, the company has commitments to purchase 2.6 gigawatts of electricity under long-term contracts, an increase from 2 gigawatts just the year before. This amount will match the energy Google consumes during a year of operations and make Google the largest corporate purchaser of renewable energy in the world — larger even than many utilities.

【198 words—*The Japan Times* (DEC 13, 2016)】

[Notes] Google：グーグル社
Alphabet：アルファベット社

86

[1]

Google (or more accurately its parent company, Alphabet) is the world's second-largest corporation by market capitalization: It is worth more than $530 billion. Headquartered in the United States, it has a digital and physical footprint that stretches around the world; in addition to office complexes that house staff and scientists, the company has huge data farms dotted across the globe.

［**Words**］ 下記の語彙について、その意味を調べましょう。

	語彙	品詞	意味
1	footprint	名詞	
2	stretch	動詞	
3	house	動詞	
4	huge	形容詞	
5	dot	動詞	

［**Phrases**］ 下記のフレーズについて、その意味を調べましょう。

	フレーズ	意味
1	or more accurately	
2	a parent company	
3	the world's second-largest corporation	
4	market capitalization	
5	be worth more than $530 billion	
6	be headquartered in the United States	
7	a digital footprint	
8	a physical footprint	
9	around the world	
10	in addition to ~	
11	office complexes	
12	data farms	
13	across the globe	

［**Comprehension**］ 本文に即して、下記の問いに答えましょう。

1. 3行目に登場する "a digital and physical footprint" とは、何を指していますか。
下記から、ふさわしいものを1つ選びましょう。

(a) グーグル社の歴代 CEO。

(b) グーグル社の時価総額。

(c) グーグル社のインターネット広告事業。

(d) オフィスビルやデータセンターをはじめとする、グーグル社の活動拠点。

【第1段落（後半）】

Those farms house massive computing facilities that consume extraordinary amounts of energy. It is reckoned that Google consumed 5.2 terawatts of energy in 2015 — the equivalent of the energy needs of the city of San Francisco or half a million homes in the U.S.

［**Words**］下記の語彙について、その意味を調べましょう。

	語彙	品詞	意味
1	massive	形容詞	
2	consume	動詞	
3	extraordinary	形容詞	
4	reckon	動詞	
5	equivalent	名詞	

［**Phrases**］下記のフレーズについて、その意味を調べましょう。

	フレーズ	意味
1	computing facilities	
2	extraordinary amounts of energy	
3	it is reckoned that ~	
4	5.2 terawatts of energy	
5	the energy needs of the city of San Francisco	
6	half a million homes	

［**Comprehension**］本文に即して、下記の問いに答えましょう。

1. 本文の内容に合わせて、空欄を埋めましょう。なお、（③）と（⑤）には数字が入ります。

- グーグル社のデータセンターには、膨大な量の（ ① ）を消費する巨大な（ ② ）が格納されている。
- グーグル社は、2015年には（ ③ ）テラワットのエネルギーを消費したと推定されている。これは（ ④ ）市のエネルギー需要、あるいはアメリカの（ ⑤ ）万世帯分のエネルギー需要に匹敵している。

①	
②	
③	
④	
⑤	

【第2段落（前半）】

[2]

In a bold move, Google announced in 2012 that it was committed to 100 percent renewable energy purchasing in its operations. This month it confirmed that it will by 2017 purchase enough green energy to meet all its energy needs.

［**Words**］　下記の語彙について、その意味を調べましょう。

	語彙	品詞	意味
1	announce	動詞	
2	purchase	動詞	
3	operation	名詞	
4	confirm	動詞	

［**Phrases**］　下記のフレーズについて、その意味を調べましょう。

	フレーズ	意味
1	in a bold move	
2	be committed to ~	
3	renewable energy	
4	by 2017	
5	green energy	
6	meet its energy needs	

[**Comprehension**] 本文に即して、下記の問いに答えましょう。

1. 本文の内容と合致するものを、すべて選びましょう。

    (a) グーグル社は、同社の事業で購入することになるエネルギーを、すべて再生可能エネルギーに切り替えると、2012年に発表した。

    (b) グーグル社は、2017年までに、事業運営に必要なエネルギーの100%を、グリーンエネルギーで賄えるようになるだろうとの見通しを、明らかにしている。

    (c) グーグル社は、2020年から、グリーンエネルギー事業に参入することを明らかにしている。

【第2段落（後半）】

> Currently, the company has commitments to purchase 2.6 gigawatts of electricity under long-term contracts, an increase from 2 gigawatts just the year before. This amount will match the energy Google consumes during a year of operations and make Google the largest corporate purchaser of renewable energy in the world — larger even than many utilities.

[**Words**] 下記の語彙について、その意味を調べましょう。

	語彙	品詞	意味
1	currently	副詞	
2	commitment	名詞	
3	increase	名詞	
4	amount	名詞	
5	match	動詞	
6	corporate	形容詞	
7	purchaser	名詞	
8	utility	名詞	

[**Phrases**] 下記のフレーズについて、その意味を調べましょう。

	フレーズ	意味
1	2.6 gigawatts of electricity	
2	under long-term contracts	
3	the year before	
4	during a year of operations	

[**Comprehension**] 本文に即して、下記の問いに答えましょう。

1. 下記の記述について、本文の内容と合致していればTを、合致していなければFを、括弧に入れましょう。

    (a) グーグル社が購入する再生可能エネルギーの量は、年々減少傾向にある。（　　　　）

    (b) グーグル社が1年間の事業で消費するエネルギー量は、3ギガワットを越えている。（　　　　）

    (c) グーグル社は、再生可能エネルギーの購入量において、世界第2位の企業である。（　　　　）

Dictation

※音声を聞いて、語彙を書き取りましょう。

[1] TRACK No. 54

Google (or more accurately its parent company, Alphabet) is the world's second-largest (^{1}　　　　　　) by market capitalization: It is worth more than $530 billion. Headquartered in the United States, it has a digital and (^{2}　　　　　　) footprint that stretches around the world; in addition to office complexes that house staff and scientists, the company has huge data farms dotted across the (^{3}　　　　　　). Those farms house massive computing facilities that (^{4}　　　　　　) extraordinary amounts of energy. It is reckoned that Google consumed 5.2 terawatts of energy in 2015 — the (^{5}　　　　　　) of the energy needs of the city of San Francisco or half a million homes in the U.S.

[2] TRACK No. 55

In a bold move, Google announced in 2012 that it was committed to 100 percent (^{6}　　　　　　) energy purchasing in its operations. This month it confirmed that it will by 2017 purchase enough green energy to meet all its (^{7}　　　　　　) needs. Currently, the company has commitments to purchase 2.6 gigawatts of (^{8}　　　　　　) under long-term contracts, an increase from 2 gigawatts just the year before. This amount will (^{9}　　　　　　) the energy Google consumes during a year of operations and make Google the largest corporate (^{10}　　　　　　) of renewable energy in the world — larger even than many utilities.

【198 words—*The Japan Times* (DEC 13, 2016)】

Useful Phrases

※下線部に留意しながら、下記の英文を和訳しましょう。

TRACK No. 56

1. The melting point of water is 0 degrees Celsius.

2. Note here that *n* is less than or equal to 50.

3. These structures cannot be observed with the naked eye.

Vocabulary Building

※音声を聞いて、フレーズを完成させましょう。その上で、そのフレーズが意
味しているものを線で結びましょう。

TRACK No. 57

1. ( ) ( ) ・	・	水質汚濁
2. ( ) ( ) ・	・	白血球
3. a ( ) ・	・	人体解剖学
4. ( ) ( ) ・	・	第一次産業
5. a ( ) ( ) ( ) ・	・	顕微鏡
6. the ( ) ( ) ・	・	内臓
7. an ( ) ( ) ・	・	活火山
8. ( ) ( ) ・	・	万有引力

Unit 13

Basic Science Research

Reading Passage

[1]

Today, government funding for scientific research is heavily distributed to projects that are expected to produce quick results and commercial benefits. Under the slogan of "selection and concentration," the basis of operation of public universities and institutions and the foundation of the nation's basic research are weakened. Ohsumi's former colleague at a research lab said the kind of research that he pursued back then may not get enough funding today.

[2]

The number of Japanese Nobel laureates since the turn of the century has reached 16, including Ohsumi — the second most in the world after the United States' 55. The award for Ohsumi, the fourth Japanese to win the prize for medicine, comes on the heels of the same prize that Satoshi Omura, a professor emeritus of Kitasato University, shared last year with American and Chinese researchers for his work on a therapy for debilitating diseases caused by parasitic worms. Like Ohsumi, many of the recent Japanese recipients have won the prizes in recognition of the work they accomplished during the days when there was sufficient support for basic research in Japan.

[3]

Ohsumi warns that science in Japan will "hollow out" unless support systems are established to help young scientists work on long-term research. He laments that scientists in Japan today face the pressure to achieve quick results "that are useful for something" such as those that can be applied to practical medical treatments within several years, but some achievements in fundamental scientific studies may not prove "useful" for another 10 or even 100 years. If scientists are under pressure to engage only in studies that can be used for some practical purpose, "genuine basic science will become extinct," Ohsumi cautions.

【280 words—*The Japan Times* (OCT 6, 2016)】

[Notes] Ohsumi：大隅良典氏
Satoshi Omura：大村智氏
Kitasato University：北里大学

[1]

Today, government funding for scientific research is heavily distributed to projects that are expected to produce quick results and commercial benefits. Under the slogan of "selection and concentration," the basis of operation of public universities and institutions and the foundation of the nation's basic research are weakened. Ohsumi's former colleague at a research lab said the kind of research that he pursued back then may not get enough funding today.

[**Words**] 下記の語彙について、その意味を調べましょう。

	語彙	品詞	意味
1	heavily	副詞	
2	distribute	動詞	
3	produce	動詞	
4	selection	名詞	
5	concentration	名詞	
6	institution	名詞	
7	foundation	名詞	
8	weaken	動詞	
9	former	形容詞	
10	colleague	名詞	
11	pursue	動詞	

[**Phrases**] 下記のフレーズについて、その意味を調べましょう。

	フレーズ	意味
1	government funding	
2	scientific research	
3	be expected to *do*	
4	quick results	
5	commercial benefits	
6	under the slogan of ~	
7	the basis of operation	
8	public universities	
9	public institutions	
10	basic research	
11	a research lab	
12	back then	

[**Comprehension**] 本文に即して、下記の問いに答えましょう。

1. 本文の内容に合わせて、空欄を埋めましょう。

今日の日本では、科学研究における（ ① ）の部分が弱体化していると考えられている。その理由としては、「（ ② ）と（ ③ ）」というスローガンの下で、すぐに結果が出て、すぐに商業的な収益につながることが期待される研究プロジェクトに、政府の（ ④ ）が重点的に配分されていることが挙げられる。

①	
②	
③	
④	

【第 2 段落】

[2]

The number of Japanese Nobel laureates since the turn of the century has reached 16, including Ohsumi — the second most in the world after the United States' 55. The award for Ohsumi, the fourth Japanese to win the prize for medicine, comes on the heels of the same prize that Satoshi Omura, a professor emeritus of Kitasato University, shared last year with American and Chinese researchers for his work on a therapy for debilitating diseases caused by parasitic worms. Like Ohsumi, many of the recent Japanese recipients have won the prizes in recognition of the work they accomplished during the days when there was sufficient support for basic research in Japan.

[**Words**] 下記の語彙について、その意味を調べましょう。

	語彙	品詞	意味
1	laureate	名詞	
2	including	前置詞	
3	award	名詞	
4	medicine	名詞	
5	share	動詞	
6	researcher	名詞	
7	work	名詞	

8	therapy	名詞	
9	debilitate	動詞	
10	disease	名詞	
11	cause	動詞	
12	recipient	名詞	
13	accomplish	動詞	
14	sufficient	形容詞	

［**Phrases**］ 下記のフレーズについて、その意味を調べましょう。

	フレーズ	意味
1	the number of ~	
2	Nobel laureates	
3	since the turn of the century	
4	the second most in the world	
5	win the prize for medicine	
6	on the heels of ~	
7	a professor emeritus of Kitasato University	
8	parasitic worms	
9	in recognition of ~	

［**Comprehension**］ 本文に即して、下記の問いに答えましょう。

1. 本文の内容と合致するものを、すべて選びましょう。

    (a) 2000 年以降、20 人の日本人がノーベル賞を受賞している。

    (b) 21 世紀に入ってからの日本人ノーベル賞受賞者数は、世界第 2 位である。

    (c) 大隅良典氏は、ノーベル物理学賞を受賞する 4 人目の日本人である。

    (d) 大隅良典氏の現在の身分は、北里大学特別栄誉教授である。

    (e) 大村智氏のノーベル生理学・医学賞は、史上初の単独受賞であった。

［MEMO］

....

....

....

....

[3]

Ohsumi warns that science in Japan will "hollow out" unless support systems are established to help young scientists work on long-term research. He laments that scientists in Japan today face the pressure to achieve quick results "that are useful for something" such as those that can be applied to practical medical treatments within several years, but some achievements in fundamental scientific studies may not prove "useful" for another 10 or even 100 years. If scientists are under pressure to engage only in studies that can be used for some practical purpose, "genuine basic science will become extinct," Ohsumi cautions.

［**Words**］下記の語彙について、その意味を調べましょう。

	語彙	品詞	意味
1	warn	動詞	
2	establish	動詞	
3	lament	動詞	
4	face	動詞	
5	pressure	名詞	
6	achieve	動詞	
7	useful	形容詞	
8	practical	形容詞	
9	achievement	名詞	
10	fundamental	形容詞	
11	purpose	名詞	
12	genuine	形容詞	
13	caution	動詞	

［**Phrases**］下記のフレーズについて、その意味を調べましょう。

	フレーズ	意味
1	hollow out	
2	support systems	
3	work on ~	
4	long-term research	
5	be applied to ~	
6	medical treatments	

7	within several years	
8	fundamental scientific studies	
9	prove useful	
10	for another 10 or even 100 years	
11	be under pressure to *do*	
12	engage in ~	
13	for some practical purpose	
14	basic science	
15	become extinct	

[**Comprehension**] 本文に即して、下記の問いに答えましょう。

1. 下記の記述について、大隅良典氏の見解と合致していれば T を、合致していなければ F を、括弧に入れましょう。

(a) 長期的な研究に取り組もうとする若手研究者がこれ以上増え続けると、日本の科学は空洞化していくことになる。（　　　）

(b) 基礎科学の研究に素早い成果を求めようとすることは、あまり意味のあることではない。（　　　）

(c) 真の意味で基礎科学が発展していくためには、若手研究者が実用的な研究のみに専念できる環境を整備していくことが必須である。
（　　　）

[MEMO]

....

....

....

....

....

....

....

Dictation

※音声を聞いて、語彙を書き取りましょう。

[1]

TRACK No. 58

Today, government funding for scientific research is heavily distributed to projects that are expected to (^{1}) quick results and commercial benefits. Under the slogan of "selection and concentration," the (^{2}) of operation of public universities and institutions and the foundation of the nation's basic research are weakened. Ohsumi's former (^{3}) at a research lab said the kind of research that he pursued back then may not get enough funding today.

[2]

TRACK No. 59

The number of Japanese Nobel laureates since the turn of the century has reached 16, including Ohsumi — the second most in the world after the United States' 55. The award for Ohsumi, the fourth Japanese to win the prize for (^{4}), comes on the heels of the same prize that Satoshi Omura, a professor emeritus of Kitasato University, shared last year with American and Chinese researchers for his work on a (^{5}), for debilitating diseases caused by parasitic worms. Like Ohsumi, many of the recent Japanese recipients have won the prizes in recognition of the work they accomplished during the days when there was (^{6}) support for basic research in Japan.

[3]

TRACK No. 60

Ohsumi warns that science in Japan will "hollow out" unless support systems are (^{7}) to help young scientists work on long-term research. He laments that scientists in Japan today face the pressure to achieve quick results "that are useful for something" such as those that can be (^{8}) to practical medical treatments within several years, but some achievements in fundamental scientific studies may not (^{9}) "useful" for another 10 or even 100 years. If scientists are under pressure to engage only in studies that can be used for some practical purpose, "genuine basic science will become (^{10})," Ohsumi cautions.

【280 words—*The Japan Times* (OCT 6, 2016)】

Useful Phrases

※下線部に留意しながら、下記の英文を和訳しましょう。

TRACK No. 61

1.　Put a small amount of sodium carbonate in a test tube.

2.　In this case, x must be greater than or equal to 15.

3.　The right side of this equation is zero.

Vocabulary Building

※音声を聞いて、フレーズを完成させましょう。その上で、そのフレーズが意味しているものを線で結びましょう。

TRACK No. 62

1.		(	) ・	・ 汗腺
2.	( )-(	) (	) ・	・ 献血
3.	(	) (	) ・	・ 気象警報
4.	a (	) (	) ・	・ 重力
5.	a (	) (	) ・	・ 生活習慣病
6.	a (	) (	) ・	・ 無機化学
7.	a (	) (	) ・	・ 赤血球
8.	(	) (	) ・	・ 大陸棚

音声ファイルのダウンロード方法

英宝社ホームページ（http://www.eihosha.co.jp/）の
「テキスト音声ダウンロード」バナーをクリックすると、
音声ファイルダウンロードページにアクセスすることができます。

**Basic Scientific English:
Starting with Newspaper Articles 2**
ニュース記事で学ぶやさしい科学英語２

2021 年 1 月 15 日　　初　版

編著者　ⓒ　鬼頭 修／安原 和也
発行者　　　佐々木　元
発行所　　株式会社　英 宝 社
〒 101-0032　東京都千代田区岩本町 2-7-7
TEL［03］（5833）5870　FAX［03］（5833）5872

ISBN　978-4-269-18053-6　C1082
［印刷・製本：萩原印刷株式会社／カバーデザイン：伊谷企画］